FEEDBACK

Strategies to support teacher workload and improve pupil progress

KATE JONES

Hachette UK's policy is to use papers that are natural, renewable and recyclable products and made from wood grown in well-managed forests and other controlled sources. The logging and manufacturing processes are expected to conform to the environmental regulations of the country of origin.

To order, please visit www.johncatt.com or contact Customer Service at education@hachette.co.uk / +44 (0)1235 827827.

ISBN: 978 1 0360 0912 0

First published in 2024 by
John Catt from Hodder Education,
An Hachette UK Company
15 Riduna Park, Station Road,
Melton, Woodbridge IP12 1QT
www.johncatt.com

The authorised representative in the EEA is Hachette Ireland, 8 Castlecourt Centre, Dublin 15, D15 YF6A, Ireland (email: info@hbgi.ie).

Typeset in the UK.

Printed in the UK.

A catalogue record for this title is available from the British Library.

Praise for *Feedback*

What a book! Whether you're an ECT or a veteran of 20 years, this is a fantastic resource packed full of ideas to help you improve pupil progress… and reduce your workload! Kate has crafted a welcoming, accessible companion that is perfect for understanding the research behind workload-saving, effective approaches you can use straight away. The case studies are a wonderful bonus, framing the advice given and showing exactly how it can be applied in a real classroom, by real teachers, across all phases of education.

If you are serious about providing effective feedback to your pupils in a sustainable manner, this is a must have on your bookshelf. It will certainly be a mainstay of our school's CPD!

Dr Daniel Rosen, head of school, Secondary at St George's The British International School Dusseldorf

Without a doubt, Kate Jones has established herself as one of the foremost experts on effective feedback strategies. Her book is a masterful guide that addresses the multifaceted nature of feedback to help move learners forward in the classroom. It is comprehensive, thoroughly researched, and immensely practical, offering a treasure trove of evidence-informed ideas for educators seeking to fine-tune their feedback and improve learning outcomes for all pupils. I'm confident this book will be invaluable to everyone in the teaching profession.

Jamie Clark, team leader: learning and innovation in a school in Perth, Australia

Kate's book takes a deep dive into the crucial role feedback plays in our students' learning. This book is highly research-informed, emphasising how the timing, content, and delivery of feedback can significantly impact a student for better or worse. Kate discusses how research can only guide us up to a point; ultimately, the final say comes down to a teacher's professional experience and smart adaptations. What I love most about the book is its practicality. Jones translates research into resources and strategies that can be easily used in any classroom. Not only are her strategies research-informed, but they also prioritise well-being. Furthermore, her book explores how technology could lighten the load if used to supplement, not replace, real feedback between teachers and students. This aspect is particularly appealing as the effective use of technology in administering feedback is not discussed enough. Overall, Kate's book is a goldmine of practical strategies. Her balanced look at feedback's complexities, along with her focus on supporting teachers and students, makes this a must-read for anyone wanting to boost learning in their classroom. As a result, I will be updating my department handbook to incorporate her strategies for administering feedback.

Emily Folorunsho, teacher of history at a secondary school in Abu Dhabi, United Arab Emirates, and author

There are several things I love about Kate Jones's new book, *Feedback*. It's worth reading for the introduction alone, which gives a comprehensive overview of what the evidence says about the impact of feedback to pupils on their learning. Each subsequent chapter gives genuine examples of how to give pupils feedback in a range of forms. Any teacher who reads this book will be able to choose a small number of feedback practices which will maximise pupils' learning and minimise teacher-effort. If I'd read this book 35 years ago, my pupils would have learned more and I would have saved myself from fruitless marking, Sunday after Sunday after Sunday!

John Tomsett, educational writer, blogger and consultant, erstwhile headteacher of Huntington Research School, York

Kate Jones has done it again with her latest book on feedback – a smashing success that seamlessly blends practicality with academic rigor. In this invaluable resource, Jones provides a treasure trove of practical examples on what to do and what not to do when it comes to giving and receiving feedback, all backed by solid research. Her hands-on approach ensures that readers can immediately apply the strategies, while her thorough grounding in academic principles ensures a deep understanding of the underlying concepts. Jones's background as a teacher shines through, as she focuses on improving education and fostering/encouraging growth. This book is an essential guide for teachers and educators, managers, and anyone keen on mastering the art of feedback. With clarity and precision, Jones has crafted a work that is both highly practical and deeply insightful. It's a must-read for anyone committed to personal and professional development in education.

Eva Hartell, educator and head of research in Haninge, Sweden

Kate Jones's *Feedback* articulates the principles that drive students forward to make meaningful improvements. The age of endless marking and low student engagement has ended – these innovative and sensible tactics give teachers the tools to develop our thinking and classroom practice. Feedback has been reconceptualised in education – this book is the guide for advancing beyond the red pen. Blending pedagogy and practice, each page is full of examples that show how we can best direct students, and empower them to make changes moving forward. Kate underlines the importance of student engagement in the ongoing dialogue between pupil and teacher. From self-assessment to questioning, from selective marking to moderation, the value of feedback is made abundantly evident, and the ease with which we can deliver feedback is a revelation.

Morgan Whitfield, author of *Gifted? The Shift to Enrichment, Challenge and Equity*

A must-read for teachers and school leaders at all levels, particularly those establishing effective feedback policy and practice in schools and multi-academy trusts. Drawing upon the best available evidence and emphasising teachers' lived experience in the classroom, Kate Jones explores the undeniable importance of actionable feedback to pupils' learning, and the importance of sustainability in terms of workload. She offers a wide range of workload-friendly strategies and practical resources to help teachers provide efficient feedback that has a positive effect on pupil progress. We will certainly be drawing upon this highly accessible book as part of our initial teacher training curriculum design and delivery.

Jo Twiby, executive director, The Exchange Partnership at Delta Academies Trust

Feedback is one of the most complex and thorny issues which exists in schools. In this new book, Kate Jones guides us through all the main forms of feedback, distilling the research and differing viewpoints. She provides workload-friendly strategies to ensure 'the juice is worth the squeeze' with feedback. The book is rooted in evidence but also classroom experience, and the case studies exemplify how the strategies can be applied meaningfully in the classroom. A must-read for anyone looking to develop their understanding and application of excellent feedback.

Rachel Ball, coaching development lead at Steplab

Kate Jones's *Feedback: Strategies to support teacher workload and improve pupil progress* is an invaluable resource for anyone who has felt swamped by the deluge of marking that often comes with being a teacher. If you've ever been told to use a verbal feedback stamp, you need to read this. If you've ever been directed to write lengthy 'What Went Well' comments and 'Even Better If' targets, you need to read this. Jones, with expert precision, challenges poor proxies of feedback and learning, whilst simultaneously offering solutions, ideas and evidence-informed approaches that can be used for progress and impact.

As an English teacher who has often felt defeated by the job ahead of me when it comes to feeding back to students, Jones's manual is an enlightening and reassuring read: the unachievable suddenly seems doable. This carefully approached and balanced account of assessment and feedback helps to clarify the intricacies of a challenging process. I expect *Feedback* to reignite the conversation around assessment and feedback, forcing teachers to not only think about what we're assessing but, more importantly, why we're assessing and what we hope to achieve by providing the feedback we do.

The problems with feedback and assessment are perpetually encountered by teachers. *Feedback* is a must-read, helping time-constrained teachers, regardless of phase or subject specialism, to face these issues head on.

Stuart Pryke, assistant principal at Iceni Academy, Norfolk, and co-author of *Ready to Teach: Macbeth*, *Ready to Teach: A Christmas Carol* and *100 for 100: Macbeth*

Rigorously researched and always relevant to the classroom, *Feedback* is essential reading for all teachers and leaders. Written with classroom teachers firmly in mind, this book has the power to change practice and redress the work–life balance crisis at the heart of teacher attrition. I wish I had this book at the start of my career.

Kieran Mackle, primary mathematics specialist and host of the Thinking Deeply about Primary Education podcast

An excellent practical guide to enhance pupils' and our own effectiveness.

Anthony Seldon, head, Epsom College

Kate Jones cleverly highlights the importance of feedback, providing an insightful focus on when and how it should be given while also not shying away from its many limitations and misconceptions. This book offers honest and thoughtful approaches to effective feedback in the classroom and how to monitor it. Using key examples from real teachers, this is a must-read for all aiming to have an impact on their students' progress, while also considering teacher workload and well-being.

Cat Chowdhary, deputy head of teaching and learning at Al Riyadh Charter School, UAE, and author

Although feedback is often cited as one of the biggest tools in our armoury, as a profession we've struggled to get to grips with how to make it effective, whilst also making it manageable in terms of workload. This book is the perfect guide to demonstrate how you can ensure that feedback can be one of your superpowers, together with easy to implement and workload-friendly strategies, without compromising on quality.

Jon Tait, director of education, speaker and author

In a time where teacher workload is often the topic of discussion, Kate has produced a timely text that goes a long way to support teachers in this area of their practice. Not only does Kate link back to the extensive research in this area, but she has used it to produce a selection of time effective and practical strategies that will support teachers and children in both the primary and secondary sectors. These strategies can be seamlessly integrated into classroom practice with a focus on what forms of feedback can have the greatest impact on pupil outcomes whether it be through verbal, written or whole classroom feedback as well as the importance of self- and peer assessment in the evaluation of these outcomes. With the support of this book, not only will the range of strategies improve pupil outcomes but it will be done so by reducing the need for teachers to feel that they need to write extensive written outcomes for children to realise that they have been successful and where they can look to improve going forward.

Adam Woodward, assistant headteacher in a primary school in Kent

Another incredibly useful book for teachers of all levels of experience from Kate. *Feedback* blends research and practical ideas in a way that means you can dip in and out on a classroom, departmental or whole-school level and come out with great solutions, whilst also ensuring you avoid common pitfalls when it comes to feedback. I will absolutely be using this to review our school's feedback policies.

Kyle Graham, assistant headteacher for teaching and learning, Golborne High School, near Wigan

Dedicated to my wonderful partner and best friend, Geoff Blythe.

Contents

Acknowledgements

I would like to thank all the contributors to this book. The authors of the case studies have spent time sharing their honest and open reflections and offering insightful advice to the readers. I would also like to thank everyone (far too many to name) who has taken the time to talk to me about feedback, ranging from their reflections, concerns, experiences, asking and answering questions and providing lots of food for thought.

My colleagues at Evidence Based Education are a great source of professional support and inspiration. A particular thank you to Stuart Kime, Jack Deverson and Jamie Scott. Michael Chiles has written and presented on the topic of feedback with a focus on evidence-based practices, so I was delighted when he agreed to write the foreword. Thank you, Michael.

The team at John Catt have continued to support me with my desire to write about education. I have a lot of gratitude for the opportunities they have provided me. Thank you to Alex Sharratt and my editor Alastair Coe.

As always, thank you to my friends and family for their continued support. The biggest and most important thank you is dedicated to my partner Geoff. Throughout this process he has supported me, from reading draft chapters and providing helpful feedback to looking after our daughter so I can have quiet time and space to read, write and reflect. I have written this book during my maternity leave, so it has not been without its challenges, but it has been a privilege to write.

Foreword by Michael Chiles

The act of giving feedback is something we do as teachers throughout the school day. It often becomes second nature to us. If we were to write down all of our exchanges we have with students it would be hard to pinpoint a time when feedback doesn't feature at some point. After all, the purpose of giving feedback to someone is to spotlight success and shine a light on the path to improvement. For this reason, it is often said that 'feedback is a gift' to embrace but all too often research shows us that the feedback we give is not always well received and therefore not actioned. When feedback isn't actioned it is unlikely that the gap between the actual vs desired performance will reduce. For this reason, the art of giving feedback should not be underestimated because no matter how well we think our feedback is delivered, students may choose not to act on it.

Our school environments continue to buzz with this gift irrelevant to its success. From feedback on following core routines to the success of work completed in lessons based on the original intentions set by the teacher. Feedback is a dominant and loud feature of schools. However, this rhythm of feedback, the flow of exchanges, the beats and frequency that happen in classrooms can easily become mismatched because the feedback is so noisy and out of tune that students end up not knowing how to act on it. The feedback can end up becoming blurry between the teacher providing it and the student responding to it.

Despite all this, what we do know from extensive research is feedback has the potential to have a positive influence on improving performance when we get it right. Shute's report on formative feedback (2007) indicates when feedback is delivered effectively it has the potential to significantly improve learning outcomes. Therefore, creating the right conditions for students to want to receive feedback is the first step which begins with creating a strong culture where mistakes are seen as part of the learning process. If we can normalise errors in our classrooms students are more likely to want to be receptive to feedback. This not only allows teachers to quickly identify misconceptions and gaps in knowledge so that they can be responsive, it also provides students with an awareness of their own knowledge gaps.

In this book, Kate Jones outlines a range of strategies that teachers can use to help reduce the gap between the actual performance vs the desired performance of students. Kate explores a wider range of feedback types that teachers can use in their classrooms, supported by the research and her own classroom experience. The approach to feedback in schools has come a long way in recent years to support learning and reduce workload. This book will provide further support for teachers who are looking for their feedback to make the right noise.

Introduction

Strategies, techniques and ideas come and go in education, but feedback has, and will continue to be, a consistent aspect of effective teaching, learning and assessment. Feedback itself is not a fad, but plenty of feedback fads have been embraced or enforced in schools.

Any element of teaching and learning can be implemented and embedded well or badly, and this applies to feedback. The effectiveness of feedback relies on a range of variables including the nature of the feedback provided as well as the level of knowledge and expertise of the pupil and their level of engagement and responsiveness. Ultimately, we have to ask if the feedback provided to pupils is having a positive impact. How do we know this and how can we check?

It is agreed among teachers and school leaders and can be seen in the research literature that feedback is an essential element of teaching and learning. Despite this consensus, there isn't a firmly agreed approach on how and when to deliver feedback. Feedback is important and can be effective, but not always. Evidence from research isn't always clear about how effective feedback can be delivered in the classroom. It remains a complex field of study.

Leading experts in this field, John Hattie and Helen Timperley, noted in their seminal paper focusing on the power of feedback (2007), that:

> Feedback is one of the most powerful influences on learning and achievement, but this impact can be either positive or negative.

Evidence can inform and support teachers, but it will never explicitly tell teachers how to teach or how and when to provide feedback to their learners. Every classroom context is unique. The application of evidence can be challenging and requires professional learning, time and reflection.

Dylan Wiliam, in the Education Endowment Foundation (EEF) Guidance Report, 'Teacher Feedback to Improve Pupil Learning' (2021), commented on the complexity of research in the field of feedback and its application in the classroom. Wiliam wrote:

> The existing research does not tell teachers how to guarantee the feedback they give their students will be effective, and probably never will; teaching is just far too complex for this ever to be likely.

Other individuals in academia and education have commented on the messy and at times confusing literature published that focuses on feedback. This is not to suggest we disregard the research; instead, as with all evidence-informed teaching and learning approaches, careful consideration and reflection is required. Teachers must use their own knowledge, expertise and professional judgement to shape the decisions and actions they take in the classroom, which is especially true with feedback.

Questions that have been raised by teachers and school leaders include the following:

Should feedback be delayed or provided immediately?

Is there a specific type of feedback that is considered to be the most effective?

How specific should feedback be?

Should feedback be written, verbal or both?

Should pupils be provided with grades, written comments or both?

Should schools take a consistent approach to feedback?

How much feedback should be provided to pupils?

How often should teachers provide feedback to their pupils?

What feedback shall I provide to my high-attaining pupils (their work is usually accurate)?

What feedback shall I provide to my pupils with learning difficulties and special educational needs?

What feedback shall I provide to my pupils who speak English as an additional language?

There is not always a definitive answer as context often trumps consistency. Feedback is the beating heart of the classroom. It is essential. Without feedback, pupils will continue to make the same mistakes and misconceptions will linger and become ingrained in long-term memory, meaning progress will be much slower or entirely absent.

Feedback has other benefits besides aiding teaching and learning, such as engaging and motivating learners to keep going and improve. Feedback is essential but it must be communicated clearly by teachers and accepted (not rejected) and acted on by pupils.

While the purpose of feedback is open to interpretation (and it is useful to discuss this) it is evident that the purpose of feedback is to improve pupils' learning – thereby improving their understanding, performance and long-term recall.

Teachers are well aware of the importance of feedback to support pupils' learning. Pupils also need to understand the relevance, value and significance of feedback. Pupils play a vital role in the feedback process. They have to be responsive to the feedback they receive but they can also provide feedback to one another through peer critique and assessment. This is not easy for learners to do; it is important to remember they are often novices when it comes to providing feedback to others. They need explicit guidance from the teacher on how to give effective feedback to their peers. Pupils also need to value, respect and respond to the feedback they receive from their peers.

Parents and carers are often interested in the feedback their child receives but without clear communication they might not understand the feedback or the methods of feedback used. Conversations about feedback need to happen at a whole-school level, among and between departments, and with parents and the wider school community of families.

Senior leaders need to clearly share their vision and aims with staff. These then need to be communicated to pupils.

When communicating feedback to pupils it is important that feedback follows the key principles outlined below:

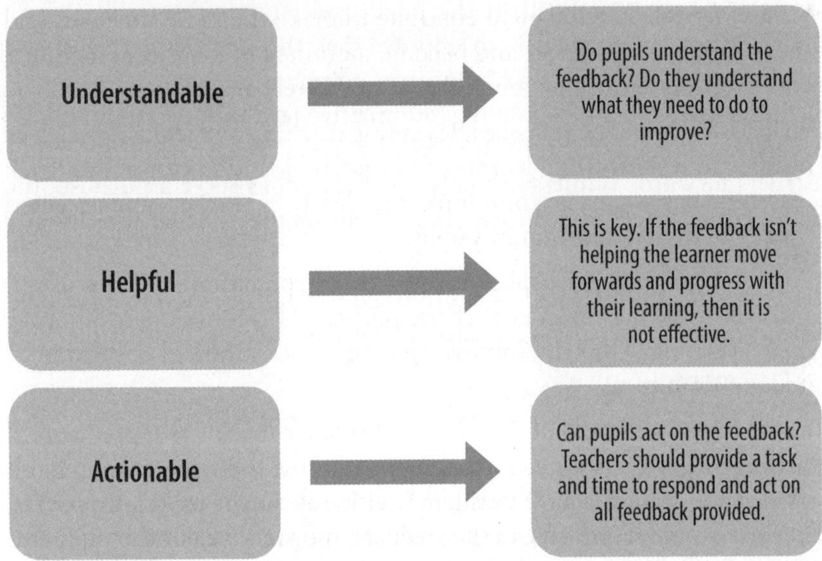

Teachers shouldn't assume pupils always understand the feedback they have received. Feedback should be clearly communicated and the teacher can check for pupil understanding. Daisy Christodoulou (2017) points out the importance of pupils understanding feedback:

> I think that for students to engage with feedback and learn from it, it needs to be understandable. They have to understand what the feedback is and that might sound really obvious, but I think a lot of feedback is really hard for people to understand.

Stone and Heen (2015) also comment on this in their book:

> Sounds obvious, seems easy. Before you figure out what to do with the feedback, make sure you understand it.

Hattie (2011) also discusses the issue with learners not understanding feedback from their teacher:

> Students often find teachers' feedback confusing, nonreasoned, and difficult to understand. Sometimes they think they have understood the teacher's feedback when they have not, and even when they do understand it they may not know how to use it.

Therefore it is vital to create a classroom culture where learners can seek clarification and ask questions about the feedback, especially if they do not understand it. If the pupil understands the feedback and knows what they need to do to improve then the feedback is useful and helpful. Feedback that isn't helpful is pointless and can leave pupils feeling frustrated and stagnating. Summative feedback is often used for evaluation, possibly for reflection too, but is not always helpful to move learners forward. While summative feedback does serve a purpose, the main focus of feedback in this book is formative, to help the learner to progress.

Teacher and author David Fawcett asked a valid question in his book, *Relearning to Teach: Understanding the Principles of Great Teaching* (2019):

> For all the time and effort, is feedback actually worth it?

This question was the focus of a chapter dedicated to feedback in his book and it is a question I have pondered on many times, especially during the early years of my teaching career. Is the juice worth the squeeze? Essentially, we need to make feedback worthwhile and meaningful. This is not always easy to do, mainly because we need the learners in the classroom to help us with this aim. The teacher can provide feedback but it is the pupil who makes it worthwhile.

Feedback provided to pupils should be actionable, allowing the learners to revise and improve. Feedback should impact future actions and therefore, by its very nature, should have clear instructions for the recipient. This is not always possible with summative feedback, such as external or end of year exams where the focus is on a final grade or judgement, but it is essential to formative feedback.

Fawcett (2019) warns:

> If we are not careful, feedback can become the end product of a piece of work. It becomes the final thing we do as teachers when the learning process is over.

A way to avoid this is through providing ongoing actionable feedback to learners and providing plentiful opportunities for pupils to act on that feedback.

The feedback strategies in this book are all ones considered to be workload friendly for teachers, but they also aim to support pupil progress and do so by being actionable. Dylan Wiliam and Siobhan Leahy (2015) have written extensively about different formative assessment strategies in the classroom, including feedback. Wiliam and Leahy write:

> The only thing that matters with feedback is the reaction of the recipient. That's it. Feedback – no matter how well designed – that the student does not act upon is a waste of time.

Teachers can invest time, effort and energy in delivering feedback but if it is ignored by the learner then all the time, effort and energy spent will have been meaningless. The response from the pupil to feedback is crucial to ensuring the formative feedback serves its purpose, helping the learner to make progress.

I recall being introduced to the concept of DIRT (dedicated improvement and reflection time) many years ago. Initially, I rolled my eyes at yet another acronym in education. I questioned how I would manage to embed DIRT into my lessons, as there was already so much to do in a lesson and a lot of curriculum content to cover. The truth is I didn't get it. I didn't grasp how important dedicated time for improvements and reflection was, and how it is a vital element of effective feedback. Planning for and providing this time is crucial. There were many lessons where I returned class books to my pupils after I had spent time carefully reading and marking each one. I instructed pupils to read my written comments but then the lesson quickly moved on and I would begin teaching new content.

On reflection, I did not give my classes enough time to engage with my written comments. I didn't check thoroughly that pupils had read or understood the feedback and I did not provide opportunities for pupils to act on their feedback. I know I was not alone doing this, and this is no doubt where the focus for DIRT stemmed from.

Paul A. Kirschner and Mirjam Neelen (2018) have identified that pupils don't often engage with the feedback they receive:

> A common problem which undermines the effectiveness of feedback, whatever type you choose to use, is that learners often don't do much with given feedback.

They add: 'A common rule of thumb here is that the more one makes use of feedback, the more effective it is.'

A key question for teachers to continually consider and be aware of when providing feedback to their classes is:

How do I ensure my pupils respond to and act on feedback?

English teacher and author Andy Tharby has written extensively about the 'Feedback loop' – focusing on the idea that feedback is a two-way process. Feedback provided to the learner can lead to improvements and close gaps in learning. The evidence from learners can and should also enable responsive teaching, so the teacher can adapt their planning and delivery when appropriate. Tharby (2016) writes:

> DIRT, when the class can begin to practise their mistakes, is a useful starting point. Too often, however, it only papers over the cracks. The most useful thing about looking at student work is that it provides us with a recipe for future action. We learn what we need to teach again or teach better; we learn about our students' working habits and how they can be improved.

Despite DIRT losing its momentum as the latest buzzword in education, the core principles of spending time to reflect, make improvements and ultimately act on feedback should not be dismissed. Specific time must be allocated for acting on feedback. Wiliam (2017) offers this advice to teachers:

> I would say as a general principle, don't ever give feedback to students unless you make the time (the next time they are in the classroom with you) for them to respond to that feedback.

If the feedback provided is understandable, helpful and actionable this increases the likelihood of pupils acting on feedback and improving. Carl Hendrick and Robin Macpherson (2017) encourage teachers to help pupils understand that they can improve as a result of acting on feedback:

> Students will only act on feedback if they believe they can get better and so motivating students to believe in improvement itself becomes a key part of the challenge.

This book includes a wide range of practical examples, resources and techniques to make sure the feedback provided is actionable. The different examples may need to be adapted depending on the age of your learners or the subject taught but the same principle of acting on feedback can be applied regardless of the context.

Effective feedback also relies on teacher–pupil relationships and communication. As teachers get to know their classes they gain a unique insight that can help to ensure the feedback is pitched appropriately in a way that can motivate and help the learner to move forwards. Wiliam (2014) stresses the importance of relationships in the classroom:

> Ultimately, when you know your students and your students trust you, you can ignore all the rules of feedback. Without that relationship, all the research in the world won't matter.

Creating a supportive learning environment with mutual respect, established routines, trust and clear communication is vital to ensuring the feedback provided to pupils is understood, accepted and acted on. Relationships and communication underpin all the strategies and techniques suggested in this book.

Workload

In terms of workload, providing feedback has to be sustainable. Teacher workload continues to dominate headlines and strike action is considered to be a result of arguably unsustainable and unhealthy working hours (among other factors including pay and funding). Workload needs to be discussed in the context of teaching and learning and the day-to-day requirements and expectations of classroom teachers and leaders.

Providing feedback is a requirement for all teachers, but it can and should be provided with realistic expectations to support teacher wellbeing and workload as well as maintaining a focus on the impact on pupils' learning and progress.

Douglas Stone and Sheila Heen note that:

> We swim in an ocean of feedback.

This is certainly true for pupils, as they constantly receive various forms of feedback throughout the school day. They are also likely to receive feedback outside of school, whether it be during music lessons or sports training, or from parents and family members. But if pupils are swimming in feedback, it can feel like teachers are drowning in marking!

The teachers' union NASUWT states:

> Excessive workload has a huge impact on teachers' health, safety and wellbeing and undermines teachers' ability to teach effectively. Four in every five teachers say that their workload and the stress of the job have increased and half of teachers say that workload has negatively affected their physical and mental health. Two thirds of teachers tell us that they are seriously considering leaving the profession because of concerns about excessive workload.

NASUWT also informs teachers that they:

> should not be required to provide extensive written comments on every piece of work, given that there is very little evidence that this practice improves pupils' outcomes in the long run.

The Teacher Workload Survey (TWS) was conducted in 2019 across England, it was a large-scale survey of teachers, middle leaders and senior leaders across primary, secondary and special schools, aiming to be nationally representative. The TWS report explained:

> The survey helps act as a national 'barometer' for teachers', middle leaders' and senior leaders' working conditions and forms a key part of the Department for Education's (DfE) commitment to improving the evidence base on what drives unnecessary teacher workload and what works to reduce it.

Although this survey was specific to England it is clear other countries are experiencing similar issues with workload in the teaching profession. Comparisons were made with the TWS previously conducted in 2016. The 2019 survey illustrated:

> The number of hours teachers and middle leaders report working out-of-school hours has fallen, both in terms of the average number of hours worked, and as a proportion of total working hours and Senior leaders also reported working fewer hours in total in 2019 than they did in 2016.

While this is a positive finding, it is evident there continue to be time-related workload issues. The report states:

> However, despite these reductions, most primary teachers and middle leaders said they still felt they spent too much time on planning, marking and data management, alongside general administrative work. Similarly, most secondary teachers and middle leaders reported spending too much time on marking, data management and general administrative work. The findings therefore suggest that there remains further work to do in reducing the amount of time teachers spend on these activities.

Providing feedback via marking has been highlighted as an area to which teachers are dedicating too much time. The TWS report found that 'teachers and middle leaders reported working an average of 12.8 hours during weekends, evenings or other out-of-school hours.' Although not surprising, this is concerning and for many teachers, feedback and marking takes place outside of school hours as shown in the report:

> Both primary and secondary teachers and middle leaders reported spending the most time on 'individual planning and preparation of lessons' (7.8 hours for primary, 7.3 hours for secondary), 'marking/correcting of pupils' work' (6 hours for primary, and 6.3 hours for secondary) and 'general administrative work' (4.2 hours for primary and 4.8 for secondary).

Feedback and marking can dominate evenings and weekends for teachers, resulting in a negative impact on teacher wellbeing and often affecting friends and family members too. This is not fair or sustainable, hence the need to focus on workload-friendly approaches to providing feedback to pupils, while aiming to deliver a positive impact on pupil progress.

School leaders are crucial to ensuring teacher workload is not excessive due to the demands of feedback and marking policies. Classroom teachers may read and engage with research about effective feedback techniques but this can be pointless if they are confined to non-negotiable whole-school policies. School policies should provide guidance to classroom teachers rather than act as shackles to practices that fail to take into consideration subject or key stage specificity. Policies should be living documents that are regularly reviewed and reflected upon, taking into consideration teacher voice, wellbeing, impact on pupil outcomes and the latest developments, literature and research in education.

Workload and wellbeing are two sides of the same coin. Through realistically tackling teacher workload, teacher wellbeing can also be supported significantly. The ripple effects of this can have a positive impact on teacher retention and recruitment.

The role of technology

Technology has become embedded as a feature of our daily lives. It has the potential to support teacher workload significantly, especially in the context of feedback. Technology has the ability to support and enhance pupil learning, helping pupils to make progress, inside and outside of the classroom, when used carefully and purposefully.

It is important to be mindful that although technology can help learners, it can also hinder their learning. It is vital that school leaders, teachers, learners (and their families) understand how technology can be used effectively to have a positive impact on teacher workload and pupil progress.

Technology is rapidly advancing, therefore anything published about the use of technology can become quickly outdated. There are also concerns about the impact of technology on the mental health and wellbeing of young people, the issue of screen time and other concerns which are explored in this book.

There are several advantages to using technology to provide feedback to learners. Technology can reduce teacher workload. There are many websites, apps and tools that can provide instant and accurate feedback to the learner; for example, in a quiz. Technology can also collect, analyse and record useful data for teachers and leaders. Another advantage with technology is that it allows pupils to receive feedback outside of the lesson, for example if they are studying at home or want to listen to audio feedback from their teacher. Technology can encourage pupils to engage with the feedback they receive and there are some tech tools which can show the teacher who has or hasn't engaged with the feedback provided.

Technology can be harnessed to provide timely and clear feedback to the teacher about the progress of their learners and can be used to efficiently communicate feedback to the pupils about their performance and progress. Technology should not be used to attempt to replace the teacher with feedback (although there are software and tools that assess and grade pupils' work without teacher input); instead it should be viewed as one of many feedback approaches teachers can use.

Although technology is advancing at a rapid pace, especially with the growth of Artificial Intelligence (AI), it is evident technology has not replaced the role of the teacher. It cannot develop relationships with pupils in the way a teacher does and often lacks the specific knowledge and insight that teachers have about the individuals in their classes. There are limitations to what any tech can achieve in the classroom. However, despite the limitations, I do believe technology can and should be embraced by teachers.

Andreas Schleicher, director for education and skills at the Organisation for Economic Co-operation and Development (OECD), shared an important message in 2020:

> Technology can amplify the work of great teachers but it cannot replace them.

The role of technology inside and outside of the classroom to support teaching and learning was transformed during the Covid-19 pandemic. Schleicher also stated:

> Online learning has changed from a nice-to-have extracurricular facility to becoming the lifeline for education.

The return to the classroom and the importance of regulating screen time has taken the spotlight away from technology slightly but lessons and skills developed during the pandemic can be used in a classroom context. Throughout this book there are examples of technology, from apps and websites, to tools such as a visualiser, with a focus on providing feedback to pupils to support their progress, while supporting teacher workload.

'Teacher Feedback to Improve Pupil Learning: Guidance Report'

I believe the Feedback Guidance Report published by the EEF in 2021 has provided much needed clarity in the field of feedback. The report states that:

> Feedback studies tend to show very high effects on learning. However, it also has a very high range of effects and some studies show that feedback can have negative effects and make things worse.

The possibility of feedback having a negative impact on pupils' progress and learning is not to be ignored. This emphasises the gravity of getting feedback right in the classroom. To address this, the report (focusing specifically on teacher-delivered feedback relevant to the teaching of pupils aged 5 to 18, within any subject area) includes six recommendations for using teacher feedback to improve pupil learning.

These recommendations are:

1 Lay the foundations for effective feedback

This is perhaps an often overlooked element of feedback, which ensures high quality teaching. Teachers have to explain key concepts, processes and content clearly and thoroughly to pupils. Feedback cannot be given to pupils until they have had sufficient time to comprehend and practise. After the teacher has elicited evidence of learning, through checking for understanding, asking questions or task completion, then feedback can be provided to learners.

This key point identifies the need for effective initial instruction to reduce the work that feedback has to do. If teachers are skilled at providing clear and rich explanations, use questioning appropriately and design effective learning activities, this can reduce the amount of corrective feedback required.

The report summarises this point:

> Before providing feedback, teachers should provide high quality instruction, including the use of formative assessment strategies. High quality initial instruction will reduce the work that feedback

needs to do; formative assessment strategies are required to set learning intentions (which feedback will aim towards) and to assess learning gaps (which feedback will address).

Hendrick and Kirschner (2024) also highlight a crucial point about teachers providing feedback to their students. They assert:

> If students don't know enough about the topic then they don't need feedback, they need more instruction.

Feedback can identify gaps in pupils' understanding, knowledge or ability to recall information from long-term memory but unless that feedback is actioned, the gap will remain.

2 Deliver appropriately timed feedback that focuses on moving learning forward

This point has the potential to be misunderstood and mutated. 'Appropriately timed' does not always mean as quick as possible. The report does state:

> There is not one clear answer for when feedback should be provided.

The report also adds:

> The evidence regarding the timing and frequency of effective feedback is inconclusive.

Again, this is a decision that has to be made by the teacher using their professional judgement. There are benefits to immediate feedback; for example, tackling a misconception to prevent it lingering. There are also advantages to delayed feedback, with greater gains in learning linked to spaced retrieval practice. There will also be times when logistics determine when feedback is provided. For example, if it is not possible to provide 'in the moment' feedback in a lesson, as pupils are using the lesson time to practise or complete a task, and if the next lesson with that particular class takes place the following week, then there will clearly be a delay in delivering the feedback.

It is important that we remember the realities of the day-to-day demands of teaching. This is particularly relevant when we consider feedback but it is rarely addressed. Sometimes, as teachers, we provide feedback when we can.

3 Plan for how pupils will receive and use feedback

This point is a central theme of this book: the importance of how pupils receive and use feedback by acting upon it. The report advises:

> Teachers should, therefore, implement strategies that encourage learners to welcome feedback, and should monitor whether pupils are using it.

The monitoring aspect is crucial. Feedback can be ignored by learners and so teachers have to ensure that this does not happen. By employing monitoring methods, teachers can review pupils' progress.

4 Carefully consider how to use purposeful, and time efficient, written feedback

The first chapter of this book is dedicated to written feedback and the different approaches that can be implemented and embedded effectively across a school. Written feedback is often considered to be 'marking', with piles of class books stacked high and teachers repeatedly writing the same comments and targets in books. However, written feedback doesn't have to be that way and certainly can play an important role in helping pupils.

5 Carefully consider how to use purposeful verbal feedback

The second chapter of this book is dedicated to verbal feedback and the different approaches that can be implemented and embedded effectively across a school. In a similar way to the chapter on written feedback, the advantages and disadvantages of verbal feedback are explored, followed by practical examples for the classroom.

6 Design a school feedback policy that prioritises and emphasises the principles of effective feedback

I was delighted to see this recommendation in the EEF Guidance Report, because as a classroom teacher, I have had to follow different feedback policies throughout my career – the good (evidence informed and workload friendly), the bad (demanding, time consuming and lacking a focus on impact) and the ugly (outrageous and outdated practices that don't help the teacher or learner!).

Providing feedback in English or humanities is very different from doing so in maths and science, as well as in art, music or PE. Feedback to young learners must be verbal, as they don't often have the ability to read and grasp written feedback, whereas older pupils may require specific feedback linked to exam assessment objectives. The report advises the following:

> Schools should design feedback policies which promote and exemplify the principles of effective feedback. Policies should not over-specify features such as the frequency or method of feedback.

Principles trump policies in a whole-school context. Policies can identify the common goals, objectives and overall approach to feedback; the practices implemented will vary across subjects and key stages.

In addition to the evidence cited, this book is also shaped by classroom experience. I firmly believe school improvement should be derived from evidence and experience. I have drawn on my years of experience in the classroom, as well as other educators' expertise. There are anecdotes and examples from my classroom and other teachers have contributed with a range of case studies. There is a danger of swamping education literature with evidence from research and neglecting teacher expertise and experience. Both are important and need to be amplified.

Feedback should be efficient (for the teacher) and effective (for the pupil). I hope this book helps teachers to provide efficient feedback that has a positive effect on pupil progress and outcomes.

Chapter 1
Written feedback

For many years written feedback has dominated school policy, and as a result has taken up a lot of teachers' precious time. There are several reasons why such emphasis and importance has been placed on written feedback, but the main arguments have focused on the recording and evidence of feedback.

Written comments recorded in books can be read and revisited by the learner, although there is no guarantee the learner will actually do this. Feedback in written form also provides visible evidence of the feedback given to individual learners for line managers, senior leaders, inspectors, parents and carers, external visitors and other interested parties.

There has been a shift away from regularly providing written comments in class books and more focus on workload-friendly, sustainable and more effective methods of providing feedback to support learner progress. However, there are many school policies that still require teachers to provide written feedback regularly, for example every three lessons or two weeks. These policies, while aiming to ensure consistency, don't capture the essence of meaningful feedback to help move learners forward.

There is an ongoing debate in education about the significance and role of marking. Marking often involves reviewing individual class books and providing written comments and adding ticks or marking codes. Marking is simply one way of providing feedback, and has historically been a widely used method. However, it is not the only method of providing written feedback. The examples of written feedback in this chapter, including marking codes, scoring and grades, and live feedback within lessons, do not involve extensive written comments.

Written feedback doesn't solely consist of the traditional form of marking, with 'two stars and a wish' style comments (the two stars focusing on two key strengths and the wish being the target) or lengthy 'WWW' (What Went Well) and 'EBI' (Even Better If) also being commonly used methods.

The EEF Guidance Report (2021) has addressed the confusion that can arise with marking as a form of feedback. The report notes:

> In many cases, written 'marking' has often been conflated with 'feedback' and may indeed have unhelpfully supplanted other forms of feedback.

The report continues:

> The review underpinning this guidance did find that written feedback interventions (which include comments, marks, or scores) are associated with improved pupil attainment when compared to no feedback or usual practice. [...] It is worth noting that written comments can be effective and should not be rejected by teachers because of the opportunity cost associated.

Schools have to carefully consider the role, purpose and impact of providing written feedback to learners while considering the 'opportunity cost', meaning the time, effort and energy required and the impact on teachers' workloads and wellbeing.

To mark, or not to mark

There are many schools that proudly advocate a 'no marking policy'. They often include this policy on the school website or within a job description when advertising for teaching positions, recognising that it can support recruitment of teachers. This may appear attractive to a teacher looking for a school that takes workload seriously, however no marking doesn't mean that feedback is absent – far from it!

The following are key points to consider and reflect upon regarding marking as a written form of feedback.

Arguments for marking

- **Accountability.** One way of ensuring learners are following instructions and investing in their work is to regularly check it. If learners are trying hard, this can be recognised and praised. If pupils have failed to complete or produce satisfactory work, this can be addressed. Checking can be carried out by collecting books and marking, though live 'in the moment' marking can also address this.
- **Learner motivation.** If learners know their teachers will be taking the time to read, review and provide feedback on their work, it can increase their effort and motivation – although this is not guaranteed to motivate every learner!
- **A record of feedback.** Written comments in individual books can act as a record for learners to revisit and act upon. Parents can also view feedback that is documented in class books. Leaders at all levels can observe feedback in books, although this can also occur without written comments, for example during an observed lesson with 'live marking' and verbal feedback.

The arguments above in favour of marking can be addressed with whole class feedback (WCF) approaches or other techniques suggested in this book. For example, with WCF, a teacher can make a note of learners who have not completed work or those who deserve praise and recognition for their efforts. There can still be accountability, and WCF crib sheets (as shown in chapter 3) can be used to record the feedback provided.

There are many teachers who do mark some work but not every single piece of it. Alternatively, some teachers opt for 'selective marking', providing feedback on specific sections of work. Other schools advocate no marking at all, with the exception of assessments.

Arguments against marking

- **It's time consuming.** This is true of both primary and secondary teaching. Primary teachers will have a set of class books to mark across all subjects with a limited amount of planning, preparation and assessment (PPA) time while also needing to plan and prepare lessons. At secondary level, although teachers specialise in fewer subjects they will have more classes across a school. This can result in the teacher having responsibility for hundreds of class books each week. There is often not enough time to mark all class books, hence why increasingly teachers mark during their evenings, weekends and holidays.

- **Is it a waste of time?** Marking can potentially be a waste of time if learners do not read or engage with the marking provided.
- **Heavy workloads.** In addition to the time taken, marking requires a lot of effort and energy. Marking often involves carefully reading individual books and providing written comments for each learner. This type of feedback is very demanding of teachers.
- **Repetition.** This is a frustrating aspect of individual marking that can be addressed with whole class feedback. A teacher may find they are writing the same or similar comments in individual books if the same factual mistakes have been made repeatedly or the same key words have been spelled incorrectly. If learners ignore the feedback and do not act on it, then the need to repeat that feedback will continue.

When reviewing these key points the focus should always be on feedback, not marking. This is an important distinction for teachers to be aware of. Marking does not always equate to effective feedback, and feedback can be provided without marking.

Sir Tim Brighouse often wrote about how the 'butterfly effect' could be applied to schools. This theory suggests that one small change can have a significant impact in the future. Building on this, school leader and experienced classroom teacher Joe Kirby (2023) has written about effective, efficient and workload-friendly teaching and learning strategies.

Kirby categorises the following different approaches:

- **Hornets** – high effort, low impact. They sting. Stop them.
- **Butterflies** – low effort, high impact. Heart-flutterers. Find them.
- **Slugs** – low effort, low impact. They are slimy. Stop them.
- **Bees** – high effort, high impact. They work. Keep them.

Marking and feedback come under different categories. Kirby describes marking as a 'hornet'. He writes:

> Written marking takes up a huge amount of teachers' time. If the average teacher marks for just over five hours a week, that's 200 hours of marking a year. In a secondary school of 100 teachers, that's 20,000 hours of marking. [...] Written marking is non-renewable; it's a one off. Each written comment I put in a pupils' book only impacts that one pupil. [...] Marking has a very low ratio of impact-to-effort and a very high opportunity cost.

Those who oppose marking do not oppose feedback. Kirby describes feedback as a 'butterfly', writing:

> Feedback is effective when it is timely (not too late after a task), frequent (not too scarce) and acted on (not ignored).

These key principles are central to effective feedback that moves learning forwards. Typically, marking is regarded as 'tick and flick' accompanied by written comments, and this practice became the norm in schools. Learners became accustomed to this type of feedback, and parents expected to see it in books. It became ingrained as a routine for many classroom teachers, and for some schools this is still the case.

When I trained to be a teacher in 2009–10 I wasn't instructed on how to provide meaningful and helpful feedback. I collected books and wrote quite generic comments, often including '*Well done*', '*Keep it up*' or vague targets such as '*Take care with spellings*'. In terms of providing feedback, I tried to recall what I received in school and looked at examples of marking by experienced teachers I encountered, and simply tried to replicate that.

As an NQT, the marking I provided to my classes was regularly scrutinised by my line manager and senior leadership team (this applied to all staff). On reflection, I realise I wasn't given any useful form of evaluation or guidance based on the feedback I was providing to my pupils. Scrutiny was there to ensure I was marking books and doing so regularly and thoroughly, but this was an accountability measure rather than one focusing on reflection and professional development.

Thankfully, the focus on feedback has changed since I trained to become a teacher. The Early Career Framework (ECF), published in 2019, states:

> High-quality feedback can be written or verbal; it is likely to be accurate and clear, encourage further effort, and provide specific guidance on how to improve. […] Over time, feedback should support pupils to monitor and regulate their own learning.

Marking is one method of providing feedback, but we have to ask if it is an effective and efficient method to provide feedback to learners. Hendrick and Macpherson (2017) comment on the use of marking in terms of providing feedback:

> A set of marked books is traditionally seen as an effective proxy for good teaching but there is a lot of evidence to say that this might not be the case. Certainly, students need to know where they make misconceptions or spelling errors and this also provides a useful diagnostic for teachers to inform what they will teach next, but the written comments at the end of a piece of work are often both the most time-consuming and also the most ineffective.

Teacher, school leader and author Greg Ashman (2015) has also written about the issues with written comments:

> Writing a comment on a piece of work is not the same thing as feedback. Instead, it is one potential way of providing feedback to students. Comments in exercise books don't even act as feedback if they are not received and the message certainly won't be received if we try to convey too many points at once or if a grade or score is also present.

Writing lots of comments in learners' books shouldn't be a reflection of the effectiveness of the teacher. I have seen this in several schools I have worked with, where teachers who spent hours marking and providing their pupils with half a page of written comments are lauded as being wonderful teachers. They are certainly dedicated and well-intentioned teachers, but were their extensive comments actually helping learners? It could be argued that their workload management should have been better. Teachers spending hours writing extensive comments shouldn't be lauded; instead, they should be encouraged to use more efficient and effective forms of feedback.

If there is a lot of written feedback and several targets for the learner to digest, this can be problematic. Firstly, it will have taken the teacher a long time to complete the marking process for a class. Secondly, the learner may not read the feedback, especially if it is considerable in length. If there are lots of areas for development highlighted, this might make it difficult for the learner to know what to focus on, which could potentially be demoralising.

Another problem with lengthy written comments is that teachers will be expected to provide learners with this on a regular basis, leading to an exhausting carousel of non-stop marking. There is advice from research studies regarding the frequency of feedback. Professors Nick Soderstrom and Robert Bjork (2015) write:

> Feedback that is given too frequently can lead learners to overly depend on it as an aid during practice, a reliance that is no longer afforded during later assessments of long-term learning when feedback is removed.

Feedback should be provided frequently, but learners will need time to act on it before further feedback is issued. Written feedback is often thought of as teachers reading, reviewing and marking books outside of the lesson. This is because of the challenge that comes with providing written feedback to every learner in a class. There often isn't enough time, but it is possible for a teacher to provide written feedback live in a lesson.

The following strategies vary, as they can be performed in a lesson or may require the teacher to review classwork outside of the lesson. Where possible, 'live in a lesson' has many benefits, for example the teacher can check that the learners have understood the feedback. This can lead to a conversation with questions and answers, and ultimately the learner can act on this. However, if the feedback is being returned to learners during the next lesson, then the time to read, reflect and act on the feedback must be factored into the lesson plan.

Marking codes

Marking codes are not new, and like most classroom techniques they can be used well or badly. When used effectively, marking codes can be a workload-friendly and quick approach to communicating errors to learners. Marking codes provide feedback to individual learners, making them aware of areas of strength or areas for improvement.

Time should be spent with learners to explain what the codes represent, using examples to make the codes clear. The codes can only be effective when learners know what each one represents and can act on them. As learners must address the marking codes and rectify errors, time should be allocated within a lesson and the corrections should be monitored by the teacher.

Author Ross Morrison McGill has written about marking codes (2017). McGill states:

> A good starting point for reducing workload is to keep marking codes as simple as possible. [...] A marking code will help feedback make sense and have demonstrable outcomes for you and your students.

In terms of literacy codes, a whole-school approach is strongly advised. The following key stage 3 example can be used across all subjects.

Literacy marking codes

You must correct the mistake highlighted by the code.

SP – Spelling error	NP – New paragraph needed
C – Capital letter required	M – Meaning is unclear
H – Homophone error, e.g. their/there/they're	WT – Wrong tense used
GR – Check and correct grammar	FS – Full stop needed
WM – Word missing	R – Repetition (word or point)
WW – Wrong word used	✓ – Correct use of literacy

Marking codes can be used to address common mistakes that can be quickly and easily pointed out to learners. Learners should have a copy of the marking codes to refer to, either in their class book or digitally (for example, via Google Classroom).

James Durran, an experienced teacher of English, media studies and drama, has warned about the impact of using marking codes for literacy. Durran (2017) writes in his teaching and learning blog:

> As with any policy or formal set of expectations, a 'marking for literacy' policy will only be as good as the reflection, discussion and training with which it is introduced and supported. Teachers and teams of teachers need to spend time understanding and agreeing what literacy means in their subject, and the implications of this for how feedback and marking operate in and for their subject.

When different departments create their own literacy version instead of a whole-school approach, this can cause confusion for learners. I recall a visit to a school where 'FS' was written in books. In one subject, 'FS' referred to 'full sentences', which was used if learners weren't writing answers in full sentences when they were required to do so. In another subject 'FS' meant 'full stop', which was used if learners forgot to place a full stop at the end of a sentence. I have seen 'P' used as a code to represent punctuation, when in another class it referred to paragraphs and in another it focused on presentation!

Using SPaG as a code for 'spelling, punctuation and grammar', for example, or QWC as 'quality of written communication' can also be vague and confusing. It is recommended to use more specific codes to identify literacy errors and areas for improvement.

If there are lots of codes used across a school, it will be difficult for learners to recall what the codes represent. If the codes are consistent then this can help learners to understand the feedback, and therefore it will be more effective and help them improve their written work. I instruct my pupils to use marking codes when undertaking peer assessment, as this gives the learners more opportunities to become familiar with the codes while they are providing feedback to their peers using the same method as their teacher.

Although I strongly advocate a whole-school approach to literacy codes, there will be examples of marking codes that are only relevant to specialist subjects. There are some codes that can be applied across all subjects, for example 'FE' ('factual error') or 'EX' ('explain your point'). There can be other whole-school codes that focus on incomplete work, reading the question carefully or presentation. Departments should liaise with one another to check if they can promote consistency and use the same codes or symbols when providing feedback to learners.

History teacher, senior leader and author Alex Fairlamb has promoted the use of codes as a form of feedback. Fairlamb (2018) writes:

> Within the remit of teaching, it speeds up marking, helps to pinpoint a level in which the students' work resides, and means that standardisation across the department can be undertaken in a much more consistent and coherent way.

The following are examples of subject specific marking codes.

History marking codes

WT – Wrong tense	J – Judgement required
FE – Factual error	QF – Question focus needed
KD – Check key date	N/D – Narrative/descriptive
NR – Not relevant	EG – Example needed
EV – Evidence required	EX – Explain your point
Ch – Chronology check	L – Link your points

Maths marking codes

WO – Working out (needs to be shown)

U – Include your units

A – Use algebraic methods

CC – Check your calculations/method is correct

R – Ruler needed

DDP – Draw diagrams in pencil

Some marking codes can be very blunt, for example 'M' being used to represent 'messy work' or a question symbol meaning that the work makes no sense. Marking codes lack any of the nuance or warmth that often comes with verbal feedback, therefore it is important to think carefully about the codes and what they represent. Teachers should also use their professional judgement to decide which codes to use on class work. An individual learner may make a lot of errors, meaning the teacher should prioritise what targets the learner needs to focus on.

Exam classes may require different marking codes that are linked to the exam specification, criteria, assessment objectives or mark scheme, but the same key principles apply. Learners must understand the codes, they should be helpful and the learners should act on the feedback explained by the codes.

Ultimately, learners should be self-assessing and proofreading work before submitting to their teacher, so they should use the marking codes as guidance to review their work prior to completion as a form of self-reflection and assessment.

Marking in the moment

Providing feedback in a lesson is something teachers do naturally and instinctively. This can occur during questioning or a classroom discussion, when walking around the classroom or in reaction to learners' classwork and answers. Live feedback and marking in the moment are discussed in chapter 2 in the context of providing verbal feedback to learners, but they can also be communicated via written feedback.

Marking in the moment does just that – it provides feedback in the moment, not in the following lesson or week. Learners need time to think, practise, apply and consolidate before receiving feedback in the lesson. There needs to be evidence of learning prior to the feedback.

There are different ways teachers can mark in the moment in a lesson, from being structured and targeted, to being responsive to the needs of learners. The biggest barriers are often class size and the challenge to write feedback in every book. Marking in the moment can be combined with marking codes, which reduces the amount of content teachers write in books while still providing valuable feedback for learners to act on.

It is worth embracing the opportunity that live marking provides to ask questions and check that learners understand the feedback and what their next steps are. It is important to encourage learners to act on the feedback as soon as possible, as they may forget it or not make the suggested corrections or improvements. This approach provides informative and helpful feedback for the teacher, who can use the insights provided from marking in the moment to plan and adapt future lessons and tasks accordingly.

Moderation marking

The purpose of moderation is to ensure that feedback in the form of marks or comments is consistent, valid, reliable and fair. Moderation can be completed with external moderators to assess the judgements that are made. One of the ways in which teachers can become external examiners is by gaining additional experience in moderating formally assessed work as an examiner. For several years, I was an external examiner at GCSE level, and moderation was a compulsory part of the marking process.

Moderation marking can also be carried out as a form of professional learning and development. This can help teachers to gain further in-depth understanding of the mark scheme and criteria. Moderation marking can potentially help teachers to identify trends and common mistakes across a sample of learners.

Moderation marking is not an approach that can be conducted for every assessed piece of work, due to the logistical challenges of staff finding the time to do so and the associated workload implications. However, despite the challenges with moderation marking, I wish I had encouraged more moderation in the department in my previous role as a head of department. Within the department, teachers collectively review specific examples of learners' work and discuss the mark, score or grade to award. There are many benefits of moderating pupil work:

- **Discussing answers/essays as a department allows for collaborative reflection.** This can include discussion of the mark scheme or success criteria.
- **Moderation can promote consistency.** This can be across a department or key stage where the teachers are in general agreement about how to award and assess work.

- **Professional development.** This process can help teachers who are at the beginning of their careers, or those teaching outside of their specialism, to gain greater understanding and confidence when assessing work.

According to the Ontario Ministry of Education (2007):

> One of the most powerful research-based strategies for linking assessment to improved instructional practice is teacher moderation. This process involves educators in a collaborative discussion of student work based on predetermined assessment criteria.

Moderation marking can be a challenge in smaller departments, but it is possible to conduct it with external teachers if the assessed content is the same. Many schools across England have become part of a multi-academy trust (MAT), and one advantage of a MAT is the option for collaboration across schools within the trust.

The Teacher Assessment Framework offers guidance and information for teachers to use at the completion stages of key stages 1 and 2. However, they are for summative purposes rather than offering learners ongoing formative and responsive feedback.

Selective marking

The selective marking approach is also known as the 'yellow box' method. Selective marking is a very simple and workload-friendly option for providing individual feedback, which is particularly useful in subjects where learners are required to write lengthy essays, such as English and the humanities. It takes a teacher a long time to mark a class set of essays or assignments – it is a challenge!

For summative assessments, such as mock or trial exams, it is important that the teacher checks all content carefully to grade it and provide feedback. However, with classwork and practice tasks, the yellow box method can be an alternative to the traditional model of marking.

The yellow box idea originated at the George Spencer Academy in Nottingham. When learners submit their written work, the teacher selects a paragraph or section to provide feedback on, as opposed to marking all the content. This section is highlighted with a yellow box, and content outside of the box is not commented upon. The box doesn't have to be yellow, although colour consistency can help learners to recognise the approach.

As the highlighted section is shorter than the whole piece of work, more attention and detail can be paid to it. Specific feedback and targets can then be provided to the learners to act upon, using brief written comments or marking codes. The learner then redrafts and improves this section, acting on the feedback provided; this isn't overwhelming for the learner as they have just one area to develop and improve. Time must be provided, either in a lesson or as an assigned homework task, for learners to improve the work in the yellow box.

There is no expectation for the teacher to follow up and review the changes learners have made (this would be heading towards triple marking territory), but it is useful for the teacher to check that learners understand the feedback and what they are required to do, as well as monitoring that learners are acting on feedback effectively at a class level.

It is important to explain the context and reasons for using this method to the learners. It is not because the teacher doesn't have the time or desire to read the full essay or answer; instead, learners should understand that this approach enables the teacher to zoom in and provide focused feedback for the learner to work on. The teacher may select the conclusion part of the essay if the learner was struggling to reach a balanced and sustained judgement. This could be a priority for a learner who needs to improve how they conclude an essay.

A yellow box (or section of a page in their class book) is provided for learners to complete, acting on the feedback by redrafting their original section. The learners could self-assess this to double check they have acted on the feedback, or they can ask a peer for support or advice. Learners can use the yellow box method when carrying out peer assessment to provide specific feedback to their classmates.

The method can work particularly well for exam classes where learners are expected to write extended answers. It is best that the yellow box is the size of a paragraph. The more text selected in the yellow box, the more time spent providing feedback and the more work for the learner to redraft, therefore defeating the purpose of specific and targeted feedback.

Ross Morrison McGill (2017) is an advocate for this approach. He writes:

> The Yellow Box is perfect for workload and supporting student progress. [...] The student knows where to work and what to target; improvements can be identified much more clearly to help aid student progress. This ensures you are marking for the child – not observers – to reduce your workload with more direct, specific comments. That leads to greater impact.

Tom Sherrington and Sara Strafford (2021) have written about the benefits for teachers adopting selective marking approaches. They offer this advice to teachers:

> Ensure that your expectations for responses are easy to act on. Do you want your pupils to answer questions, redraft, correct spellings or develop their ideas in more depth? Set clear, manageable goals and plan time for students to respond. This method works as a really effective starter or plenary activity and could even be set for homework.

English teacher Dr James Alsop (2019) has written about the use of the yellow box as a method of providing feedback to pupils. Alsop writes:

> The Big Yellow Box completely changed my marking process, and made it better in every conceivable way. Not only did deployment of this strategy make it possible to zip through essays and homework in a fraction of the time, but it made my marking far more effective. The Big Yellow Box gives students greater agency in responding to feedback and improving their work, and enables teachers to monitor progress with accuracy.

As a teacher of exam classes for both history and politics, I have found the yellow box approach to be very helpful. My learners responded well to it as they were able to focus on a specific area, improve and master that, then move on to another aspect of improvement.

A variation of the yellow box method involves the teacher asking questions linked to classwork for the learner to answer in the blank yellow box. Another twist on this approach is to ask learners to select the paragraph or section of work they want the teacher to focus upon. The learner may select a paragraph they believe to be their strongest and feel most confident about, or they could select what they consider to be their weakest section, aiming to improve it using the feedback provided. If learners do not have errors in their work, a yellow box can be created to add further detail, discussion or explanation.

A note of caution: if learners are told in advance that only one section of their work will be reviewed by the teacher, they are likely to dedicate more time, effort and concentration to that part in comparison with the rest of the work. To combat this, learners should be told once the task has been completed that they can select the yellow box area.

While the yellow box method is quicker than traditional marking, it will take longer than a whole class feedback approach. The resulting benefit is the individual feedback for learners, but the trade-off can be the extra time required to carry out the method. The teacher should make a call using their professional judgement. This is a technique that can be used in some cases, but in other situations a teacher may prefer whole class feedback. It does not have to be one or the other; it can depend on the task and where learners are in the learning process.

Successful snapshots

The 'successful snapshots' technique is directly linked to the yellow box method, however it is important to ensure learners understand the difference between the two. The yellow box is an actionable task, whereas the snapshot's purpose is to highlight a key strength or section, thereby demonstrating excellence.

When using a selective marking approach, teachers tend to select the weakest paragraph or section for learners to then improve. It is possible to identify strengths in the yellow box that has been selected, but the focus tends to be on the corrections required. For the teacher to focus on the weakest part of classwork and not recognise or address the strongest part can understandably be frustrating for the learner.

The successful snapshots approach, is similar to the yellow box, as a section of work will be 'boxed off' by the teacher, but this box is used to highlight areas of strength and success. It is best to use a different colour pen to ensure a distinction between the yellow box feedback, which learners are expected to rework and improve. The snapshot box doesn't require further improvements; it is simply there to add recognition and praise.

Learners do not have to do anything with the classwork in the snapshot box. The actionable feedback comes from the yellow box method. Learners can be asked to reflect on and answer the following question: *Why do you think that section of work was picked as the successful snapshot?* This allows learners to review and reflect on their work, identifying the areas of strength.

This method can also be used with peer assessment, where learners have to select a section, answer or paragraph as the snapshot. They can then explain to their classmate why that section is strong.

Redrafting

As an experienced author I am well aware of the importance of redrafting. It is a vital part of the writing process to improve the overall quality of my work. To redraft I regularly review my content in order to self-correct and improve. I also seek feedback from colleagues or my partner, in addition to my editor, during the redrafting process. By the end of the redrafting process the writer should be happy with their finished piece; I am always pleased with the progress from the first draft to the published content!

Learners can also develop the skill of redrafting from a young age and should be able to transfer this skill across a wide range of subjects and topics. There can be different areas to focus on when redrafting, from improving literacy errors (including a wider range of vocabulary) to adding more depth, detail, explanation or examples. The purpose of redrafting could be to make the piece of work more interesting for the reader or to alter the structure. Overall, the main aim is to improve accuracy and quality.

Redrafting is an actionable task for learners to improve a piece of classwork based on feedback (from the teacher or peer), but we must remember the advice from Dylan Wiliam (2016) that feedback should improve the learner not the work. It can be daunting and time consuming for a learner to redraft a whole essay, so focusing on specific sections or paragraphs can be more manageable and help to improve the learner's skill set, not just their work.

Redrafting tends to lend itself to essay-based subjects, but any lesson where learners are expected to write a paragraph or more can involve redrafting and improvement.

If learners are unsure about how to redraft their work, the teacher can share a sample piece of work (provided with permission from the learner and ideally anonymised to avoid any potential embarrassment). The teacher can use a visualiser, or learners can be given the sample piece of work to annotate. The teacher can then model different ways in which the piece of work can be improved to the class by highlighting areas or elaborating on points.

This activity can be completed as part of a 'think, pair, share' task. Learners can review the sample material individually, trying to find any mistakes or areas for improvement as well as areas of strength. Following the individual thinking time, learners can discuss the work with their partner and they can swap and share their views and suggestions. For the final part, the teacher can call on learners to share their feedback with the rest of the class.

Learners can spend time reading and redrafting a sample piece of work. This is useful practice to prepare them for redrafting their own work using the same approach and principles. Learners need to fully grasp that redrafting work doesn't always require adding more content; indeed, the exact opposite could be the case. Redrafting may involve reducing the amount of written content by making points clearer and more concise, for example by removing unnecessary words or repeated points.

Redrafting work isn't always a valuable use of time for learners, or the teacher. There are many ways in which redrafting can be ineffective, for example when learners spend time rewriting a whole essay or lengthy piece of work for very little change. The overall presentation may improve (perhaps a missing full stop is added, or a spelling is rectified), but there has to be a significant difference and improvement seen when redrafting.

On redrafting, Tom Sherrington (2017) writes:

> Redrafting is very powerful provided that the actions are very specific and the scale of the task is manageable for both teacher and student.

Ideally, redrafting should take place before work is submitted to the teacher, with edits and improvements based on peer feedback or self-checking and correcting. (See chapters 4 and 5 for more advice and guidance on self- and peer assessment methods.)

Learners can use success criteria to monitor their own progress and redraft their first attempt. Redrafting is a great example of actionable feedback, but to ensure it is an efficient use of time for both the learner and teacher there should be a visible and significant improvement from the original piece of work compared with the redrafted version. This can only be achieved when learners understand how their work can be improved, therefore the feedback from the teacher or peer must be understandable, helpful and actionable.

Asking learners to redraft or rework a whole task can also be time consuming for the teacher if they need to provide feedback again. A better idea is for the learners to redraft a specific section. This section could be identified by the teacher or selected by the learner or a peer, as demonstrated in the yellow box method. This means that learners don't have to rewrite all their classwork but can instead focus on specific sections or paragraphs to improve. Redrafting should focus on the learner improving, not just improving the work.

Comparative judgement has become more widely used and discussed in education in recent years. This trend has been evident in teachers sharing their reflections on social media and presenting at educational conferences, as well as in the way technology has been used to support comparative judgement.

Daisy Christodoulou, author and director of education at No More Marking, is a strong advocate for the use of comparative judgement in education. Comparative judgement can have a significant impact on improving the accuracy of assessment, in addition to supporting teacher workload. Christodoulou (2018) explains:

> Comparative judgement offers a way of assessing writing which, as its name suggests, does not involve difficult absolute judgements, and which also reduces reliance on prose descriptors. Instead of markers grading one essay at a time, comparative judgement requires the marker to look at a pair of essays, and to judge which one is better. The judgement they make is a holistic one about

> the overall quality of the writing. It is not guided by a rubric, and can be completed fairly quickly. If each marker makes a series of such judgements, it is possible for an algorithm to combine all the judgements and use them to construct a measurement scale. [...] In the last few years, the existence of online comparative judgement engines has made it easy and quick for teachers to experiment with such a method of assessment.

After seeing Owen Bryan-Williams post on X (formerly Twitter) about using comparative judgement to assess learners' work, I asked him if he would be willing to explain this further with a case study. Bryan-Williams provides the reader with context, explanation and key reflections about the use of comparative judgement to assess learners' work.

Case study: using comparative judgement to assess learners

Bio: Owen Bryan-Williams is the head of history and politics at a secondary school in South-West London. His X social media handle is @mrbwteach. You can find out more about No More Marking via their website: https://www.nomoremarking.com/

In my experience the spring term is the toughest for marking and feedback. Multi-paper mock exams are being held for years 11 and 13, NEA (non-exam assessment) marking is underway and KS3 are completing their termly assessments. It was against this backdrop that I decided to try comparative judgement.

Comparative judgement is a method of assessment based on the direct comparison of two pieces of work. The main principle behind it is that humans find it difficult to make absolute judgements, i.e. placing a single object in a particular category (e.g. dark, long). Absolute judgement is particularly difficult when it comes to marking extended writing. This is because the mark schemes we use are vague – what's the difference between 'good knowledge' and 'wide-ranging knowledge'? Furthermore, while it's likely that you and I have a good idea what the difference between those two descriptors means in practice, it's unlikely that we have the same idea.

What humans are better at doing is comparative judgement. This is where two objects are compared to each other (e.g. darker, longer). When it comes to marking, the question that is asked when comparing two pieces of work is simply, which is better? This is not a new idea – it dates back to the 1920s and the work of psychologist Louis Thurstone. More recently Daisy Christodoulou and David Didau have advocated for the wider use of comparative judgement in education.

With mock exams and coursework piling up I decided to give comparative judgement a try on my KS3 assessments, the last part of which was a piece of extended writing. The method I followed consisted of three stages.

1 Read each answer individually and allocate it to one of three categories: top, middle or bottom

I used the 'first principles' of evaluation, analysis and evidence when making this decision. I read the whole answer, but it was a quick judgement – no more than 30 seconds. I purposefully didn't have a pen with me, so I avoided marking the scripts. The answers were then laid out in three long rows in a classroom. If this sounds like absolute judgement, then you'd be right. It was one of the compromises I had to make to gain efficiency. However, in the second stage I could (and did) move some scripts out of their initial category.

2 Rank the answers within the categories from top to bottom

After the first stage certain themes had emerged, for example in Year 8 (when we were studying the resonance of Elizabethan England in the twentieth century) the use of statistics about the size of the Spanish Armada and the Luftwaffe were a sign of a high level answer. When I came to reread the responses in the second stage I was often looking for the presence or absence of such relative indicators and moving the script appropriately in the rank – including between categories if necessary.

3 Allot marks

My aims when allocating marks were twofold. First, I wanted to produce a spread of marks so I could differentiate between students – there is no point in every student getting 10 out of 10 on a summative assessment. But second, I aimed to produce a high average of marks (around 75%) to give as many students as possible a sense of success and motivate them to work. So I gave the top five students 10 out of 10 and the next five 9 out of 10, and so on. The caveat being that if the answer was just a sentence or two, or even a blank page, then a lower mark (including zero) could be applied.

I then took photos of all the scripts I had marked and made a set of slides to share with the rest of the department as a guide for their ranking. Later, spot-checking helped to further improve consistency.

In the most sophisticated models of comparative judgement, each piece of work is compared at least 10 times by multiple markers to get a consensus view on its relative strength. Complex algorithms are then used to produce scaled marks. My version of comparative judgement is much simpler and cannot claim similar levels of accuracy to those used by experts in this area of assessment. But since the accuracy of comparative judgements are far higher than that of traditional absolute judgements, I feel my 'home-style' version is not substantially worse than using a mark scheme. Certainly, I am confident that the work at the top of my rank is better than that in the middle, and likewise the work in the middle of the rank is better than that at the bottom.

Having said that, there are ways to improve the accuracy of my method. For instance, if you could enlist another teacher to do the comparisons with you, that would help. Similarly, if the whole cohort could be compared en masse, instead of by class, there would be an improvement in consistency too. But the provision of exemplar answers (the photos of my ranking), plus the spot-checking, act as two further safeguards to the teacher-by-teacher method of comparative judgement.

I have only used this method on KS3 assessments. This is because I am wary of using comparative assessment on GCSE and A level papers where an 'official' way of marking exists (i.e. the exam board mark scheme).

The main advantage of my version is that it's much faster than both traditional absolute judgement and more sophisticated versions of comparative judgement. I could get through a class of 30 scripts in about an hour after school. The benefits of this are obvious. First, an exhausted teacher cannot teach effectively, and, in my view, marking is the primary workload problem teachers face.

If early careers teachers are encouraged to use comparative judgement as part of their assessment tools, then burnout may be avoided. For more experienced teachers like myself, the use of comparative judgement frees up some time to produce more resources. For example, I have been trying to increase my use of quizzing and I've been able to put some of the time saved towards creating new question banks to use for retrieval practice.

The efficiency of comparative judgement doesn't mean feedback can't be given. But recently I have been trying to separate summative and formative forms of feedback and so the only mark on each script was the score. Having said that, the process of comparison revealed the strengths and weaknesses of both individuals and the class as a whole and therefore comparative judgement can be combined with whole class feedback or individual intervention.

Looking back, I feel that this trial with comparative judgement was a success, and I will continue to use it, but only in lower school assessments for now.

Mark schemes

Mark schemes are particularly relevant to exam classes at key stages 4 and 5, as examination boards provide mark schemes to assist with assessment and feedback. However, other key stages may use mark schemes with practice SATs questions and papers, for example, or mark schemes created by teachers.

Generic mark schemes can be helpful, but it is important to remain aware that they are often designed to support teachers, not learners. Mark schemes are also created for summative assessments (to provide an overall judgement with a mark, level or grade) and do not offer actionable feedback for learners.

Some exam boards create learner-friendly mark schemes, though a teacher can adapt the mark scheme to make it more appropriate and therefore more helpful for learners to refer to. Mark scheme grids combining levels, scores and descriptors can help pupils understand where they are in terms of their performance and what they need to do next to achieve higher marks or reach the next level.

Once again, becoming an examiner can provide a teacher with further insight and understanding of the mark scheme and how scores and grades are assigned.

Although I argue, like many others in education, against lots of written feedback provided to individuals, this is not the same as advocating the removal of written feedback. When learners receive a grade or score alongside written feedback, they tend to focus on the former and are more likely to ignore the latter, which is the formative element aiming at helping students to improve.

If their grade or score is high (or they are satisfied with it), then the learner may become content that they have done a good enough job and will aim to do the same next time, although there are very likely still areas for improvement. If a learner has a low grade or score they can feel demoralised, demotivated and disappointed – this can cause a 'what's the point?' attitude. Both of these scenarios are not helpful because either way the learner isn't engaging and acting on the feedback provided.

This raises questions about whether teachers should provide grades, scores or comments to learners when providing feedback. Below is a case study from experienced teacher Paul Cline, asking whether we adopt no more marking, or no more marks.

Case study: no more marking, or no more marks?

Bio: Paul Cline is a psychology teacher and director of teaching and learning (former head of department) based in Suffolk. He is on X @PaulCline_psy.

Marking and feedback is a complex beast, and one that represents a huge proportion of teacher workload. There have been significant shifts in thinking in recent years towards a more feedback driven model rather than most teachers' traditional conceptions of what marking looks like. This has been guided by research such as that described in the EEF report (2021) on effective feedback. One issue remains a problem, still, in many places: the insistence on giving students a mark or grade on every or most pieces of work. The research here is equivocal; the EEF report states that:

> Written methods of feedback, including written comments, marks, and scores, can improve pupil attainment; however, the effects of written feedback can vary.

In my own mission to make the marking and feedback I do more effective, one cornerstone for me has been to remove marks or grades from the process almost completely. I'm reflecting on this from a psychology perspective, and I am referring mostly to extended responses or essays. That said, I do think many of the arguments outlined here will apply to many other subject domains and be relevant for short answer questions too. I think there are a several reasons to support withholding of marks (or just not giving them at all).

1 Scores are not very reliable

Marks don't help students improve. I don't trust my own marking. I've attended enough external in-service education and training (INSET) over the years to know that I won't reliably score answers the same way as examiners. Even trained examiners work to a 'tolerance level' of disagreement which is fine when scaled up across the whole qualification but more significant when it's just one piece of work. What if I give it 9 out of 12 and another colleague reads it and suggests 8 or 10, or 7 or 11? There's no objective way to determine who is correct, and I might even change my own mind on a second reading (we've all been in those standardisation meetings, right?).

At what level is a student 'happy' with this discrepancy? Furthermore, exam boards don't work to a consistent standard year-on-year. Feedback from mark schemes, examiners reports and training courses shows that they change their criteria over time (or, rather, they change the nuances of the way those criteria are interpreted and applied to learners' answers). What might have gained a 7 out of 8 in 2017 might only have scored 5 out of 8 in 2019.

It's virtually impossible to avoid inherent biases while marking. It might be possible to anonymise work to some extent, especially when marking in large volume, but then it's less easy to give personalised feedback. Over time we get to know learners' handwriting or sometimes even phrasing and we are no more able than anyone else to avoid the effects that our knowledge of particular students has on our judgement of their work. We are also biased towards what we've taught them – we look for particular things that we've mentioned in lessons. It's like a nice bit of validation for our teaching, but that's not to say that examiners would credit them in the same way.

2 Scores or percentages might be useful indicators but grades are not valid

Exam grades are calculated holistically on the basis of a much larger sample of the domain (across several exam papers) so there's no meaningful way to extrapolate a score on a single piece of work to a 'working at' grade. Analysis of exam performance across papers and cohorts shows that learners rarely perform consistently on extended answers. So while it might be true that if they typically score, say, 80% on essay questions then that is likely to lead to an A* grade, virtually no student actually performs this way in real exams.

But this extrapolation is what learners and teachers do all of the time. They either figure out for themselves (based on analysis of some grade boundaries), or teachers tell them, that 75% is equivalent to, say, a grade A and then apply that rule to all pieces of work, no matter how many marks it might be worth. I think most teachers understand this problem but don't communicate clearly enough, and learners (or parents) don't listen.

When a teacher says, *This essay is A grade standard*, what they really mean is: *If you wrote consistently to this standard, under exam conditions, on every question that comes up on the exam, then, based on some educated guesses about likely grade boundaries (which can't possibly be known in advance), which I'm basing on the limited number of exam series that have happened since the start of this iteration of the specification (and don't forget the massive disruption caused by Covid), it's very likely that your score would probably be enough to get you an A.*

What the learner hears, of course, is, *You got an A.*

What about where we give grades on the basis of larger assessments? We might set an assessment for a particular unit and then give it a grade on the basis that it represents a more significant sample of the domain and therefore such extrapolation is valid. This is not true. When we give students a test, we aren't wholly (or at all) concerned with what it tells us about their performance on that test, rather what conclusions it might allow us to draw about how well they might perform with material that wasn't on the test (i.e. the final exams). The more that the content of the test is predictable (i.e. they know what will be on the test to a decent degree in advance), then the less valid those inferences become. Therefore, the kind of smaller assessments that students typically complete throughout the year (e.g. end of unit tests) are not valid indicators of future performance because first the domain sampled is too small, and second the content of the assessment is too predictable.

3 Scores on individual pieces of work don't tell students 'where they are'

Answers are too often completed 'open book'. This is not a real indication of what students can actually do for themselves and is rarely completed under timed conditions. We might get around this by confining our marks to only those pieces completed in class where we have better control over the conditions under which they are completed. This represents a significant time investment, though, and for subjects with significant amounts of extended writing in their exams it is hard to balance time for such practice with the demands of curriculum coverage.

However, whether completed at home or in class, they are often scaffolded to some extent (possibly quite heavily) by teachers first (e.g. writing a plan together beforehand, on material literally just covered), which again makes the work completed unrepresentative of real exam answers. To be clear, I think we should be scaffolding their answers in advance by sharing success criteria, giving models of excellence or completing planning together. These are all helpful to learners, but they reduce the usefulness or meaning of any marks we may then assign to their work.

As noted above, marks on exam paper questions are designed to reflect the conditions under which the answers were written. Unsurprisingly, many students are capable of producing very high scoring answers in their own time, which bear no relation to what they might produce under exam conditions. Many students write way more than they possibly could in the time given during exams. You can't award 'bonus' marks, so how do you explain or identify at what point the answer has done enough to hit top marks? This may be possible with points-based questions, but often does not apply to an extended response where you might need to see where the learner 'arrives' at the end of their answer before making a judgement on the quality of their overall argument.

4 Scores or grades on single pieces of work rarely help students improve

What are learners actually meant to do with this information? As noted above, if it doesn't really tell them 'where they are' with any real degree of accuracy, then how does this information help them get better (beyond the motivational prod of realising how below standard their answers might be, although we can achieve this in our feedback without giving scores)?

As with grades, the presence of numerical marks decreases the likelihood of learners engaging with any feedback comments, which means that number is not going to help learners get better. As one teacher commented in a staff survey we conducted on marking and feedback at our school: Most students are not bothered about listening to feedback – once they've got their mark – as they are either chuffed and not bothered, or cheesed off and not in the mood to listen!

Some students might hold a 'threshold' mark in their heads – the score which to them is deemed acceptable. This is based on flawed extrapolation from marks to grades (see above) and may lead to complacency or an unwillingness to engage with feedback. If you get 12 out of 16 on an essay and you 'know' that this equates to an A grade, and you need an A to get your university place, then why bother trying to make it any better? On the other hand, if the only information you've been given is how to get better, then that's all you can respond to.

Extended answers are typically scored using level-based marking, which often means a holistic judgement rather than simply awarding 'points' across different assessment objectives and then adding them up (even if this is what some examiners might actually do in reality). This makes it really hard to be able to quantify how students might improve. If someone gets 6 out of 12 we can easily tell them very specific things to improve, but there's no way we could accurately and reliably tell them how to make it a 7, or an 8. The mark becomes a distraction because learners are trying to figure out how much they need to improve rather than just how.

Similarly, the way questions are written and marked means there is not one 'right' way to produce a particular answer. Two answers that 'feel' very different might score similarly, and it's very hard to explain clearly to students how and why this is. This also means that advice about looking at answers that scored higher than your own can, without very careful teacher input, be unhelpful as learners are unlikely to be expert enough to discern what they personally need to do to improve.

Stop giving marks and grades. Simple, right?

There are times, of course, when giving a mark or grade is appropriate. When learners have completed work under authentic exam conditions, we believe it does truly reflect that students' capability. When they have been assessed on a significant sample of the domain (e.g. mock exams). When they're considering their future options and need a rough benchmark of potential attainment to guide their choices. But beyond these specific, and infrequent, situations, there is probably little merit in it.

However, there are problems with applying this philosophy in a personal capacity if it's not supported by and reflective of the whole-school culture. If another teacher in your department continues to score or grade, then you are definitely the bad guy. If you're the only teacher refusing to give a mark or grade, then teachers may presume you're the one doing it wrong. Even worse, this view may well be echoed among senior leaders. If your school reporting cycle requires an attainment grade that is closely coupled with performance in an assessment, then it can be hard to explain to students the extent to which their grade has been informed by that assessment, rather than it being a direct translation of their score. This underlines the importance of devoting time and training to improving assessment literacy in all staff, especially senior leaders.

To summarise:

- Giving marks or grades in most circumstances is simply too unreliable or unhelpful to be worth the time or effort.
- Where it is necessary to award marks or grades, teachers and schools need to communicate clearly, and consistently, precisely what that information does and doesn't actually mean.

Spelling strategies

Feedback is an essential aspect of literacy. If incorrect spellings are not identified, learners will naturally continue to misspell words. Spellings can be checked through self- and peer assessment, in addition to teacher checks. A quick and visible method of identifying incorrect spellings is the use of literacy codes, as discussed previously in this chapter. Spelling errors can also be discussed with whole class feedback.

Highlighting an incorrect spelling is important, but it's essential that learners take note of this feedback and act on it by spelling words accurately in the future. There are online tools to support learners' literacy, such as the spell checker feature in Word and Grammarly, but these tools improve the work, not the learner.

A research paper published in 2015 by Professor John Dunlosky and his colleagues compared two common methods of spelling instruction. It concluded from the results that retrieval practice was a more useful and engaging training method to enable better spelling. Therefore, an actionable task should be for learners to have the opportunity to practise recalling the spellings of key words from memory.

Spelling tests often take place regularly in primary schools, but they can and should be carried out in secondary schools as well, across all subjects. A 'do now' or retrieval practice task tends to focus on the recall of knowledge, but these tasks can also be an opportunity to rehearse and retrieve spellings from long-term memory. The spellings learners have to remember can be tier three vocabulary (sophisticated and subject specific terminology) or words that have been identified as difficult.

An issue that can occur with spelling tests is where learners perform well on the test but later revert to spelling the words incorrectly in their written work. This could be due to the learners cramming. If learners study the spellings close to the test or quiz, through crammed revision, this enables them to retain the correct spelling but only in the short term. Learners must use spaced retrieval practice for long-term learning. Teachers should repeat quizzes to give learners the opportunity to recall information and spellings more than once from long-term memory. This can help learners to master spellings and develop confidence with their literacy skills.

A commonly used spelling strategy involves the teacher (or peer) identifying a spelling error by using the literacy code 'SP'. This is followed by an instruction such as 'x3', which requires the learner to write out the correct spelling three times. The aim of this is to provide learners with an opportunity to act on the feedback provided by practising spelling the word correctly. However, learners must make every effort to ensure that when they write the key word they do so accurately. Writing the word correctly does not guarantee that learners will be able to remember to spell it accurately in the long term, hence the importance of regular practice, rehearsal and retrieval with spellings.

The SAMR model (2010)

In the field of educational technology (or 'edtech'), the SAMR model has become established and widely discussed. SAMR is an acronym and framework, coined by Dr Ruben Puentedura in 2010, which represents substitution, augmentation, modification and redefinition. Although technology has advanced significantly since 2010, the principles of SAMR are still relevant and applicable today. We can also consider SAMR with a focus on feedback.

Substitution – technology acts as a direct tool substitute, but there is no functional change

Writing an assignment on a digital document in contrast to paper (without any features such as spell checker) is a direct example of substitution. Using digital flash cards instead of paper is another example, as the purpose is the same (to answer questions by recalling information from long-term memory) but the digital option reduces the need for paper and is more practical and accessible for learners. Digital flashcards can also provide immediate feedback to learners, in the same way that a double-sided flashcard can.

An example focusing on feedback can include learners completing a multiple choice quiz using an online app. The app will provide feedback to the learner to let them know if their answer was correct or not. A teacher could also provide this feedback to learners in the lesson by reading out or presenting the answers to the class. The app offers a substitution in the approach to feedback.

Jackson Best (2020) has written about the SAMR model, explaining:

> Substitution strategies can save you time and space by cutting back on laborious pen and paper tasks. Instead of printing out twenty-plus paper resources that clog the cupboard, you can use technology to manage resources with just a few clicks.

There may seem little point in using technology as a substitute, but it can support learning, reduce teacher workload and could be a more environmentally friendly option.

Augmentation – technology acts as a direct tool substitute, with some functional improvement

At this point the technology should bring some further benefits, and begin to enhance teaching and learning rather than just substituting a traditional approach. An example of augmentation might be the use of visual aids and video to support teaching new concepts and help learners to understand content.

In terms of feedback, learners could complete a paper quiz outside of the classroom and use an answer sheet to self-check, or the feedback for the quiz can be provided to the class during the next lesson. However, with the use of technology learners can complete quizzes outside of the classroom and receive immediate feedback. The feedback and scores online can also be viewed by the teacher, so that the teacher can adapt their next lesson. This offers some improvement and extra advantages for both learner and teacher.

Dr Serhat Kurt (2023) writes:

> At its heart, augmentation enhances the original task with a technological boost. It's like giving a textbook the ability to interact, showcase multimedia, and even provide real-time feedback. The primary focus here is on amplifying the learning experience, leveraging technology to introduce elements that wouldn't be possible with traditional tools. The critical reflection for educators during this phase is, 'Does the technology add new features that improve the task?'

Substitution and augmentation are considered to be strategies to enhance teaching and learning, whereas modification and redefinition are considered to be transformational to teaching and learning.

Modification – technology allows for significant task redesign

At this point in the SAMR model, technology will be creating opportunities for the teacher and learners that would be difficult to achieve without the use of technology. An example of this can include a virtual learning environment (VLE) or platform where learners can access class materials, resources, tasks, feedback and further information online.

An example of this is Google Classroom. Through using Google Classroom, the teacher can communicate with their classes and provide instruction, support and feedback either at an individual, group or whole class level. Learners can have access to lesson presentations and worksheets, which can support learners who were absent or wish to revisit lesson content.

Redefinition – technology allows for the creation of new tasks that were previously inconceivable

Although redefinition is the final part of the SAMR model, this is not necessarily a goal to work towards. Redefinition refers to anything that would not be possible without technology, which includes innovative and engaging ideas and strategies.

Best writes:

> Remember, redefinition isn't the same as 'high tech'. A learning experience is redefined when it integrates technology seamlessly and meaningfully to open new doors for student learning – regardless of how sophisticated that technology might be.

Vibbl and Teacher Fast Feedback are both examples of redefinition. Learners would not be able to listen to the audio feedback from their teacher (provided by Vibbl) without the use of and access to technology. Teacher Fast Feedback has found a way to transcribe and print verbal feedback to save teachers time while still providing learners with a record of the feedback from their teacher. Again, this would not be possible without technology.

There are digital tools that can assess learner work and provide feedback without the input of the classroom teacher. Clearly, there are benefits and drawbacks to this approach, and there are questions to be raised about accuracy, reliability, ethics, privacy and the overall impact on learning.

Jennifer A. Kingson, journalist and author, has blogged about how teachers in the US are using AI to provide feedback to their classes. Kingson writes about a tool called Writable, which uses ChatGPT to assist grading and assessing pupil work. Kingson (2024) writes:

> Teachers use [Writable] to run students' essays through ChatGPT, then evaluate the AI-generated feedback and return it to the students. [...] A teacher gives the class a writing assignment – say, 'What I did over my summer vacation' – and the students send in their work electronically. The teacher submits the essays to Writable, which in turn runs them through ChatGPT. ChatGPT offers comments and observations to the teacher, who is supposed to review and tweak them before sending the feedback to the students.

Kingson also refers to teachers using AI to hold learners to account:

> Teachers are already using ChatGPT and other generative AI programs to craft lesson plans, syllabuses and curriculums – not to mention grading papers and checking students' work for AI-enabled plagiarism and other forms of cheating.

The SAMR model can help teachers to consider the 'why' and 'how' when it comes to using technology. Dr Serhat Kurt explains the potential impact of SAMR, writing:

> The SAMR model acts as a beacon for educators, nudging them to contemplate their decisions around incorporating technology in their lessons. It pushes them to delve deep into the rationale and methodology behind each tech inclusion. With consistent engagement and reflection, teachers find themselves not just becoming tech-savvy, but also refining and advancing their instructional methods.

In terms of feedback, we can use technology as a direct substitute, which serves a purpose in reducing teacher workload. Other tools and apps can provide feedback to learners in an innovative way that is understandable, helpful and actionable and would not be possible without technology.

How can artificial intelligence (AI) support teachers in the classroom?

AI can support teachers in various ways in the classroom, enhancing the educational experience for both educators and students. Here are some ways AI can be beneficial:

Intelligent Tutoring: AI-powered tutoring systems can provide real-time assistance to students, helping them with homework, practice problems, and test preparation. These systems adapt to students' progress and provide targeted feedback.

Grading and Assessment: AI can automate the grading process, saving teachers time and reducing the risk of bias. It can also provide detailed analytics on student performance, helping educators identify areas that need improvement.

Content Recommendation: AI can recommend educational resources and materials, such as textbooks, videos, and interactive simulations, to teachers and students based on their specific needs and preferences.

Classroom Management: AI can assist in managing classroom logistics, such as scheduling, attendance and communication with parents. It can also help with behaviour management by identifying potential issues and suggesting appropriate interventions.

Language Support: AI can aid in language instruction by providing pronunciation feedback, offering grammar and vocabulary assistance, and even facilitating language translation for students with different native languages.

Special Education Support: AI can be particularly valuable in providing support for students with special needs. It can offer speech recognition for non-verbal students, assistive technology for those with physical disabilities, and adaptive learning for those with learning disabilities.

Data Analysis: AI can process vast amounts of educational data to identify trends, patterns, and insights, which can help educators make data-driven decisions to improve teaching methods and curricula.

Professional Development: AI can recommend relevant professional development opportunities for teachers, based on their individual goals and areas for growth.

Administrative Tasks: AI can handle administrative tasks, such as managing schedules, sending reminders, and handling routine communications, allowing teachers to focus more on teaching.

Parent–Teacher Communication: AI-driven communication tools can facilitate regular and effective communication between teachers and parents, keeping them informed about students' progress and any concerns.

Classroom Assistance: AI can serve as a digital assistant within the classroom, answering questions, providing information, and helping with instructional tasks.

It's important to note that while AI can offer valuable support to teachers, it should not replace the essential role of educators. Teachers bring a human touch, empathy, and real-world context to the classroom, which are crucial for a holistic and effective educational experience. AI should be seen as a complementary tool to enhance teaching and learning, not as a substitute for the teacher–student relationship.

The answer to the question on page 66 was generated by AI, through the online service ChatGPT. The prominence of AI does raise important points for teachers to consider, such as supporting teacher workload, the potential to enhance learner progress and removing factors such as teacher bias when marking and grading assessments.

In August 2023, Arran Hamilton, John Hattie and Dylan Wiliam published a working paper entitled 'The Future of AI in Education: 13 things we can do to minimize the damage'. The authors identify in the abstract:

> In all the hype about AI, we need to properly assess these risks to collectively decide whether the AI upsides are worth it and whether we should 'stick or twist'. This paper aims to catalyse the debate and reduce the probability that we sleepwalk to a destination that we don't want and can't reverse back out of.

The paper contains 13 recommendations suggested by the authors as to how developments in AI could be regulated to 'slow things down a little and give time for informed choices about the best future for humanity.'

The paper goes on to explore the various benefits and concerns raised by AI within the context of education. One of the benefits identified is the reduction of teacher workload. The authors identify the different ways in which AI can support teacher workload, including providing feedback to learners. But this comes with a warning:

> Such technology could substantially enhance the effectiveness of educators, while also giving them much-needed work–life balance. It could, of course, also significantly erode professional expertise – with teachers and lecturers expertly reading their lines but not knowing why particular approaches work.

Despite the concerns listed, the main issue highlighted is that of future education and learning. The paper is a detailed discussion and exploration of AI in education.

There can be errors or issues with feedback not being clear or appropriately pitched to support learners when using AI. The teacher must be involved in using any form of technology to provide feedback, with regular monitoring, checking and overall approval and quality assurance being necessary. There should also be transparency with learners about how feedback has been provided.

To find out more about AI in education I recommend teachers subscribe to Teacher Prompts. This informative newsletter was launched by educator Neil Almond in 2023, and its aim is to help teachers learn about, keep up with and harness the power of AI. There are regular blogs, articles and links to events and evidence focusing on AI in education. It is a fantastic resource to learn about and stay up to date with the latest developments, debates and discussions around AI. To sign up visit https://news.teacherprompts.ai/

Chapter summary

- There is a time and place for providing written feedback to learners without marking individual books and repeating comments and targets.
- There are efficient methods that can be carried out in the lesson, such as marking in the moment and using marking codes.
- Selective marking methods allow learners to receive individual feedback they can act on while being a quicker and less time-consuming alternative to traditional marking.
- Technology can be harnessed as a method of providing effective and efficient written feedback.
- The key principles of effective feedback apply to written feedback: learners should understand it and it should be helpful and actionable.

Chapter 2
Verbal feedback

The first type of feedback children receive in their life is verbal. This will likely be from their parents, carers or family members as they learn new skills, from walking to talking. Verbal feedback is the first type of feedback learners are given when they begin school, and they will continue to receive verbal feedback throughout their education and likely for the rest of their lives.

Providing verbal feedback to pupils happens naturally and is something teachers do instinctively every lesson, every day. Although it happens organically, it is still important to reflect on the verbal feedback provided and ensure pupils listen, understand and act on it. Pupils need to understand that dialogue is essential to verbal feedback; it is not about being passive as the teacher reels off targets. The pupils have a responsibility to engage with the teacher providing feedback.

As with all types of feedback there are benefits and drawbacks, pay-offs and trade-offs. There are many benefits to using verbal feedback, including the following.

- **Live feedback.** Verbal feedback can be carried out during a lesson, in the moment, as the pupils are working, and it has the potential to have an immediate impact on pupil performance and progress (in contrast to delayed feedback).
- **Clear communication.** Verbal feedback can lead to interesting and useful conversations with pupils about their understanding, knowledge, skills and overall learning. Learners have the opportunity to ask questions or seek clarification (this is possible with written feedback but easier to do during a verbal conversation).

- **Workload friendly.** Verbal feedback doesn't require teacher time or effort outside of a lesson (although this may be needed when providing recorded audio feedback).
- **Tone.** This can be misunderstood or missing with written feedback and is naturally much easier to convey and communicate verbally.

The potential drawbacks of verbal feedback include the following.

- **Forgetting feedback.** Due to working memory capacity (working memory is limited in terms of how much information can be stored and how long it is stored for), pupils may quickly forget the feedback or guidance they have received from the teacher. Unlike written feedback, there is often no record for the pupil to refer to. (This is discussed further, later in this chapter.)
- **Are students listening?** There is no guarantee pupils will read the written comments in their books, but there is also no guarantee pupils will listen and act on verbal feedback (but in this case it can be easier for the teacher to recognise if a pupil is not listening or engaging).
- **Challenges with one-to-one verbal feedback.** Although verbal feedback is less time consuming than providing written comments, it can be very difficult for the teacher to ensure each individual in the class receives verbal feedback during a lesson, especially where large class sizes and other factors such as lesson timings can be a hinderance.
- **Recording verbal feedback.** It can be difficult to measure or evaluate the impact of verbal feedback. Leaders or teachers may have a concern about the lack of visible evidence inherent to verbal feedback, but clearly the real evidence is the progress pupils are making.

An article published in the Harvard Business Review (2022) suggests when it is appropriate to provide written feedback and when it is better to provide verbal feedback. In summary, it argues written feedback should be provided when:

- There is enough time to do it right.
- You want to reinforce or capture what's been said in a conversation.
- You want to give the other person time to process it first.

According to the article, spoken feedback should be given when:

- The feedback is more complex.
- There are difficult emotions involved.
- Your goal is to strengthen or repair a relationship.

This advice is not specific to educators but does offer some valid points to consider. The first point highlights the importance of time when providing written feedback. This is something all teachers need more of – time is precious and sparse! Written feedback does allow the receiver to read and process but this can also be achieved with verbal feedback if pupils are given time, and the goal is explained clearly and thoroughly.

Feedback is often personal and can be emotive. Teachers can demonstrate kindness and empathy, but it is much easier to communicate through spoken feedback with other factors such as tone, eye contact and body gestures. Tone and emotion are harder to convey in written comments. The Harvard Business Review article further states:

> We often avoid giving feedback because we fear it will hurt the relationship. Clear and thoughtful feedback can actually have the opposite effect and strengthen the bond – if it's a conversation. This is because good feedback is collaborative. When you take time to listen to the other person's perspective and work together to find solutions, you can end up coming to a place of deeper mutual understanding.

Relationships between the teachers and pupils, and also among classmates, are important in the classroom. Feedback, if delivered with kindness, respect and honesty, can be used to strengthen and develop relationships.

The EEF Feedback Guidance Report (2021) recommends the use of verbal feedback in the classroom, but a valid point about verbal feedback is raised:

> Regardless of how it is delivered, it is crucial to note that verbal feedback is not simply an 'easy' alternative to written feedback. While it may offer a time-efficient alternative to some forms of written feedback, careful thought and consideration is still required when delivering it.

Through lesson observations with colleagues or the use of video software tools, teachers can reflect on the verbal feedback they provide to their learners. There will be verbal feedback provided that is responsive and live in the lesson, but there will also be opportunities for the teacher to provide prepared verbal feedback, either to the whole class or to individuals.

Verbal feedback has perhaps not always received the recognition it deserves, in terms of its place in the classroom, due to a strong desire to demonstrate 'evidence'. Written comments provide evidence that teachers have marked books and provided feedback to their pupils, but that doesn't necessarily equate to evidence of learning and progress. Pupil progress with attainment and achievement, in an academic sense with knowledge, skills and understanding but also with pupil confidence and wellbeing, should be the evidence all stakeholders in a school community focus on.

The concern about verbal feedback not always being considered as valuable as written feedback has been explored in research. A study published in 2020 focused on how secondary teachers' oral feedback in whole class interactions is received and perceived by the pupils in the classroom. The study is summarised as follows.

> The study examined perceptions of teachers and students in English and mathematics classroom interactions. Key findings showed that much teacher feedback was not recognised by students, and that when feedback was recognised it was often not perceived as the teacher had intended. [...] Further, feedback in mathematics was more often recognised and perceived as intended compared to English. If feedback is not received by students, or not perceived as intended by the provider, it is unlikely that the feedback message will achieve its intended effect of supporting student learning. The study provides evidence that feedback perceptions – and thus feedback effectiveness – are context-dependent, subject-dependent, and individual-dependent.

The interactions that occur in the lesson are very valuable and should be viewed that way by all stakeholders. Communication is key in a classroom, especially with feedback.

This book includes a range of feedback strategies and techniques that move away from lengthy written comments in books. However, to truly move away from this form of feedback (and embrace verbal feedback), school leaders at all levels should be leading by example and guiding staff towards efficient, effective and evidence-based approaches.

The following is a case study by a school leader at a leading international school in the United Arab Emirates (UAE). This school has embraced an evidence-based feedback approach, focusing on workload-friendly strategies to support pupil progress.

Case study: Leading a whole-school evidence-based and workload-friendly approach to feedback

Bio: Nigel Davis is the head of secondary at the British School Al Khubairat in Abu Dhabi. He has been in senior leadership positions for 15 years, both in the UK and in the UAE, with the main focus of his work being teaching for learning and establishing practices within teaching that truly get the best out of all learners.

Nigel has a master's degree in education, and is a founding fellow of the Chartered College of Teaching. He is passionate about teacher collaboration and is one of the founders of the Abu Dhabi Teaching Conference, a free annual conference for teachers across the Middle East that attracts over 500 teachers each year.

From a school leadership perspective, you are often wrestling with different agendas, and the lens through which you view a particular challenge will dictate how you approach it. Feedback is one of these; often, school leadership can take a broad-brush stroke and hold everyone in the system to the same standardised method of feeding back, where accountability is easily checked off, for example, by marking books every two weeks and having them scrutinised to check up on this. This could be seen as creating consistency; however, it can also be a glass ceiling for effective feedback.

We were far more interested in having a truly successful process for feedback (and just as importantly, impactful reflection from pupils that came as a result of the feedback) than we were in having a process that allowed us to 'check up' on staff. We also believe that if you look after staff (by means of their wellbeing, but also their professionalism), allowing them to feel valued, allowing them to grow as professionals, then the pupils' results will take care of themselves. Great teachers, by their very nature, have a deep-set desire for all learners to achieve their very best; therefore, if the teachers are given the freedom and trust to deliver the very best, then this will be their aim – as opposed to a tick box exercise of 'doing some marking'.

We therefore put together a whole-school 'feedback and reflection' policy, followed by bespoke departmental documents produced by each department. The whole overarching policy was a high-level set of reasoning behind our drive for feedback and reflection. This includes the need to think carefully and plan for the type of things that you will be looking for (using the 'backwards design' principles from the book by Jay McTighe and Grant Wiggins, *Understanding by Design* (2005)), and then following the guiding principle from Dylan Wiliam, that 'feedback should be more work for the students than the teacher.' Feedback should cause the pupils to think about their work and how to improve it, and their thinking should be related to the learning goals that the teacher has planned and shared with them, meaning the teacher needs to provide the time and expectation that the pupil does something with their feedback.

After sharing this philosophical vision of why feedback and reflection is such a vital part of the learning process, we challenged the heads of department to produce their own bespoke 'feedback and reflection statement' document for their subject areas. They were provided guidance on how this would look and its structure, but also given autonomy over what it would contain.

We asked for statements on three different types of feedback: ongoing feedback within the classroom (what this looks like to someone coming into the room); key items within each scheme of work (for consistency across the department, in the planning stage it is best practice to agree on some more structured formative assessment opportunities); and the feedback of summative assessment, so there is a formative use for these summative assessments.

We also requested information on how subject areas would encourage reflection on their feedback, both of ongoing feedback and also for more summative assessments. Demonstrating the planning of reflection within schemes of work was seen as vital, as this is the practice that can often be missed by staff.

These documents belonged to the department areas. This is important. This means that they own them, have agreed to them, and therefore hold themselves to account for what they say. Senior teams showing trust in department areas is very powerful. Our line management meetings are opportunities for heads of department to demonstrate the benefits of their own way of doing things to the learning process, so it is driven from the classroom up, rather than an accountability measure from the top down. The school also has a detailed oversight of what is happening throughout the school and is able to show this to any inspection team.

What is most important though, is that what is happening within classrooms really works. We know that a one-size-fits-all approach to different disciplines will not work across the board, as truly impactful feedback (and reflection) happening one way in French does not look the same as truly impactful feedback (and reflection) in mathematics. Many subject areas continue to use traditional written responses, whereas several (and increasing numbers) of areas are using digital methods for feedback, for example audio and video opportunities that pupils can save for future reference. Verbal feedback is also recognised as a key approach to providing feedback to pupils, across all key stages and subjects.

> Although the setting up of this takes time – it is a process that took two years, and only now does it reduce workload – there is no expectation for 'marking books', as we know that feedback is planned for carefully and is actioned by pupils to allow for far more powerful learning.

I was a head of department at the British School Al Khubairat until 2021, and was therefore involved in the 'feedback and reflection' approach described in this case study. I found this approach to be very helpful and empowering as a teacher and leader.

Verbal feedback and working memory

When it comes to the issue of forgetting verbal feedback, what are the solutions?

When individuals become frustrated because they have forgotten the name of a person they were just introduced to, or they can't remember what it was they were looking for when they entered the room, these issues can be attributed to working memory. Working memory can be frustrating because it is unreliable and limited in terms of how much information can be held and for how long for. Dr Amishi Jha (2021) explains:

> Working memory capacity is really the ability to hold and manipulate information while you're actively trying to block out distraction.

Dr Susan E. Gathercole and Dr Tracy Packiam Alloway (2008) compare working memory to a sticky note. This is a useful metaphor to use when explaining the limitations of working memory to pupils. A sticky note is limited in its capacity, as it can only hold so much information and is naturally a temporary resource. A sticky note isn't a secure and long-term storage space – it's more of a holding zone.

In 2021 the EEF published a report summarising the latest evidence for cognitive science approaches in the classroom. One of the main findings from the report states:

> Cognitive science principles of learning can have a real impact on rates of learning in the classroom. There is value in teachers having working knowledge of cognitive science principles.

The report also emphasised the importance of educators understanding the processes by which individuals commit information to memory, and this includes the role of working memory. The report explains:

> Many of the strategies derived from cognitive science focus on the crucial interactions between working memory and long-term memory and the important observation from cognitive science that our working memories have limited capacity.

Teachers should be aware of the limitations of working memory when providing verbal feedback to learners. The teacher shouldn't give the pupil too much feedback, for example several targets to focus on. One or two specific targets are better for the learner. By talking to the pupil about the targets, they are processing the information, meaning they can hold on to that information in their working memory for longer.

It is also helpful for the pupil if they are given actionable feedback that they can act on immediately, as that information will be held in working memory. For example, the teacher may inform the learner that they have forgotten to add full stops at the end of their sentences. If the pupil simply acknowledges the feedback and the teacher moves on, they may continue to do their work and forget the feedback, not correcting their work and continuing to write without full stops. If the pupil addresses the feedback immediately, checking and correcting their work, the feedback will have made a positive impact and is more likely to be retained.

If a pupil is regularly repeating a mistake or reinforcing a misconception despite regular feedback from the teacher, another idea is for the pupil to make a written record of the feedback in their book to refer to.

Verbal feedback with Early Years Foundation Stage

The benefits of verbal feedback are evident across subjects and ages. However, for younger children verbal feedback is vital as it is the only method of feedback they can understand until they develop their reading and writing skills.

The EEF Feedback Guidance Report (2021) does not include advice for educators in Early Years Foundation Stage (EYFS), noting:

> Early years is not included as the underpinning systematic review found little relevant evidence in the area.

However, the EEF has published an Early Years Toolkit. This toolkit is designed to support EYFS professionals with their decisions and lesson planning to improve learning outcomes for younger children, particularly those from socioeconomically disadvantaged backgrounds.

The statutory framework for EYFS (effective from January 2024) covers all group- and school-based Early Years providers in England (including maintained schools, non-maintained schools, independent schools, free schools and academies) and all group-based providers on the Early Years Register. The framework focuses on the importance of communication and language, which includes reading, storytelling, conversations and questions, in addition to providing feedback to young learners.

The framework also stresses the importance of verbal communication and spoken language with young children:

> The development of children's spoken language underpins all seven areas of learning and development. Children's back-and-forth interactions from an early age form the foundations for language and cognitive development.

I have had the privilege to observe an EYFS classroom. I was amazed at the enthusiasm, interactions, questions and curiosity demonstrated by the children. Feedback again plays a central role in the learning, development and growth of learners.

The following case studies by Louise Vann and Kerry Lynch offer interesting and informative insight and guidance about feedback in an EYFS context.

Case study: Feedback in EYFS 1

Bio: Louise Vann is an experienced Early Years practitioner who is currently working as an Early Years leader and reception class teacher at Muscliff Primary School, Bournemouth.

It was great to take this opportunity to reflect on how feedback looks in an Early Years setting and the different types of feedback that are communicated to young learners. In our setting we have worked hard to find the delicate balance between teacher-led learning tasks and child-led learning. Feedback for young children needs to be clear, immediate and at the point of learning for them to be able to connect the feedback to the learning that has taken place.

This can be quite straightforward during a teacher-led task. For example, in writing we are working on forming a simple sentence using capital letters, finger spaces and full stops while using the phonemes we know to spell words. Working with small groups, I can quickly identify any improvements needed and support them to improve or practise this. I use actions to go with things they need to remember (for example, for a capital letter we pat our head twice) to help support recall.

This is more challenging during child-led learning tasks and takes a great deal of skill from the adult, which is often the part which isn't recognised by an outside observer. In fact, most of our training this year has focused on effective adult interactions using Early Years practitioners such as Julie Fisher and Gregg Botrill to guide this.

During child-led learning we want the children to engage in deep level learning, which happens when they are deeply involved in the activity they have chosen. This is a crucial part of early childhood development and part of the 'characteristics of effective learning'. Teacher feedback is less straightforward in these situations as there is no clear learning intention; we must use our knowledge to tune in to what the child's next steps might be.

Many times, I have bulldozed into some child-led learning with my preconceived teacher feedback questions, only to be given the cold shoulder or disrupt the flow of learning which has then been abandoned by the child. I have learned that careful questioning and timely interactions are the name of the game. Usually, watching and waiting for a child to speak to you means they have given you the golden ticket to enter their play. It is then up to the practitioner to quickly think about where that child is, what that child needs and what opportunities there are to move learning forwards. This is all skilfully done on the spot and in the moment. Of course we don't get it right every time, but when we do it is magical.

Recently, during 'let's explore' time, I watched a group of children set up four chairs just outside the role-play area. I quickly realised this was a car and I decided to get in and ask where we were going. Thankfully the children told me we were going shopping. I seized the opportunity to introduce some mark making into the play (fine motor development and pencil control being a target for two of the children) by telling the children that we needed to make a map.

The children looked at me blankly. One of the boys then rescued me by telling me that his dad had a map on his phone. Of course, no one uses paper maps anymore! We spent the rest of the afternoon making laptops for the car. I was able to support two children concerned with their scissor control and provide bespoke feedback on holding their pencils correctly and formation of some letters, as well as lots of other skills in all areas of learning.

I am very lucky to have a supportive senior leadership team who are invested in our approach to Early Years. I also don't ask my team to do copious amounts of unnecessary recording of observations – I would rather they spend the time with the children. A truly enabling environment can result in an Early Years practitioner having about 1,000 interactions in a day. These can be as small as supporting a child to do their coat up or longer interactions over a period of time. Each one provides golden opportunities to provide skilful feedback that moves learning forward.

Case study: Feedback in EYFS 2

Bio: Kerry Lynch is originally from North East England but is now working internationally, and is currently a classroom-based deputy head in an all-through school. She has worked in Early Years education for approximately 17 years. You can connect with Kerry and check out photos of learning environment classrooms on Instagram as Allthingsearlyyears.

Feedback in education and specifically in Early Years has evolved dramatically. When I trained, feedback given to young children was still written in books. Yes, four-year-olds had books to record in, and not just in literacy and maths. It didn't really seem to matter that the children couldn't read it. I remember asking why we needed to write down feedback while training, though I never actually got an answer. The feedback was often framed as '2 stars and a wish' in an attempt to make it child friendly. I am pleased that feedback has evolved and changed into something that is more child centred.

The foundation stage has gone through many evolutions, sometimes with positive outcomes and sadly sometimes not. Much research has been done on brain development and how play supports neural pathways. This has impacted how we guide and support children. In terms of feedback, it has thankfully been a positive move. It is no longer a diluted version of KS1, or even KS2!

Feedback is now done more holistically and should be part of everyday practice. Giving both positive and negative feedback provides children with information and helps them adapt their behaviour, correct errors, refine skills and promote metacognition as well as self-regulation.

In my current school we teach in the moment; there is a constant loop of observation, teachable moments and next steps with the children. This cycle could take a minute or be a longer exchange. Feedback is a huge part of the teachable moment.

Recently, some of my boys were building a model of the Burj Khalifa and it kept falling down. They couldn't figure out why. I stepped in and wondered why this was happening. This gave them a second to pause and think, and I showed them a photo of the Burj Khalifa and pointed out the base of it. With support they could see it was larger at the bottom. They then worked with some guidance to create a solid foundation for their building. The feedback was relatively subtle and allowed them time to think for themselves and develop a solution.

One of the lovely things about feedback is the building of confidence and self-esteem. When children receive positive feedback, they can develop a sense of competence that motivates them to try harder and persevere when faced with a challenge. However, positive reinforcement should be specific, for example, 'I liked how you shared your bike, that was super kind.' One of my biggest bugbears in teaching is when I hear phrases such as 'super job' or 'good work' – it is well meaning, but unfortunately meaningless.

One of the biggest buzzwords in Early Years today is 'self-regulation', which feedback can certainly promote. Positive feedback reinforces the desirable behaviour, while constructive feedback encourages children to think about their actions and understand how to improve. One of the key factors here is how the adults model regulation skills. Our own behaviour and attitude is incredibly powerful with our little people.

Overall, we have genuinely progressed with feedback, and best practice is now more in line with how little minds work and is done in a manner that is constructive and supportive, enabling children to move forwards in their learning journey and truly thrive.

The Verbal Feedback Project

For many years I have followed the work and content created by Ross Morrison McGill, ranging from blogs to resources and books. McGill has been a loud and proud advocate for workload-friendly and evidence-based teaching and learning approaches. Feedback is an area in which McGill has specialised, and he was involved in the Verbal Feedback Project, published in 2019.

Run by the University College London (UCL), the project was designed to explore and evaluate the impact of verbal feedback approaches on the outcomes of disadvantaged students in years 7 and 8. McGill states the rationale for the project:

> In my opinion, the perception that 'written feedback is king' and that it is a mark of hard work is something that needs to be questioned and put to bed. [...] Our findings suggest that verbal feedback, when applied well, has a positive impact on the engagement of all students (and gains in progress and achievement) and – at the least – appears to have no detrimental effects.

The report summarises the key findings:

> Verbal feedback is not a single intervention; it is better defined as a complex series of refinements to practice. Very many of the participating teachers reflected on the challenges of 'unlearning' their usual approaches and implementing verbal forms of feedback which were novel to them. For that reason teachers, departments and schools that are inclined to move over to verbal feedback ought first to consider the professional development implications of such a move.

Marking can be a hard habit to kick! After years (or decades) of extensively marking books, to shift from that to an increased use of verbal and whole class feedback can be challenging, as illustrated in the summary of findings from the report. The Verbal Feedback Toolkit (2019) also offers further advice and reflections about the use and impact of verbal feedback in the classroom.

Live feedback

Monitoring the classroom and observing pupils can be multifaceted. It can be carried out as a behaviour technique to ensure learners are focused on the task and not distracting others, and it can be an opportunity to praise, motivate and encourage learners. Another benefit of monitoring is the opportunity to view pupil work, ask questions and provide feedback in the lesson. It can be a challenge to talk to every pupil in a lesson, but not every learner requires further support, challenge or feedback.

The Flying High Partnership published a research report in 2018 that focuses on reducing teacher workload. As part of this research topic, six different approaches to reduce marking workload were trialled within 16 schools across one term. One of these approaches was 'marking in the moment', specifically with targeted verbal feedback. The publication reports:

> 'Marking in the moment' focused on providing immediate targeted verbal feedback to pupils in lessons to reduce written marking. Six schools (48 teachers) used this method in English and maths, with some teachers supplementing verbal feedback with symbols for additional prompts or to identify which work had received verbal feedback. [...] Each school aimed to target two groups in a lesson for verbal feedback and then minimally mark the other pupils' work as necessary. In the original survey, teachers in this group reported spending between 2–18 hours marking.

The six feedback approaches were measured using the same research methods: surveys, interviews, focus groups, reflection journals and data reviews. The results from the survey illustrate that:

> Most of the teachers returning the final survey (18/20) reported that it lessened their marking workload; some described this as 'drastically reducing marking', but two said, 'It had less of an impact than I hoped', due to their previous use of verbal feedback to supplement written marking. All wanted to further develop this method to include more subjects and devise other ways to increase its effectiveness for pupils. Teachers described

> the impact on pupils as increased confidence, self-esteem and motivation, and better progress.

One of the teacher's reflections revealed how they used a 'clever choice' of seating arrangements to enable other children to listen to the feedback conversations. Another reflection added that:

> Some children enjoyed the chance to make improvements during the lesson, but others felt it was distracting, so this had to be taken into account.

It can be helpful for the teacher to keep a record of pupils they have supported and provided feedback to. This can simply be a tick on a register. This can help the teacher to ensure all pupils are provided with verbal feedback either in the current or following lesson. If the teacher identifies several pupils making the same mistake, then a whole class approach to verbal feedback can be provided to avoid repeating conversations with learners.

There are lots of ways in which teachers can provide live feedback in a lesson, such as a feedback conversation, asking questions to encourage reflection and the 'detective strategy', which can be an effective method to ensure learners act on the feedback in the lesson.

The detective strategy

The detective strategy is a great way to ensure that pupils are acting on feedback provided to them, rather than just being presented with it. This idea is credited to Dylan Wiliam and Siobhan Leahy (2015), and can be easy to implement during a lesson. The concept is simple: instead of the teacher telling learners where they have gone wrong, the teacher gives some feedback and guidance but the pupils have to find and fix the errors themselves. The feedback is a task, a mystery or a problem to solve.

The following example includes five questions a pupil has answered during a maths lesson. The teacher is circulating in the classroom and informs the pupil that two of the answers to the five questions need to be corrected.

Task: Solve the equation to find x

1) 4x + 3 = 51 Answer = 12
2) 6x – 2 = 28 Answer = 5
3) 12 + 5x = 62 Answer = 10
4) 7x – 3 = 53 Answer = 9
5) 5x – 1 = 64 Answer = 12

The pupil then has to return to their answers, double check, find out which two are wrong and correct them. This is the find and fix technique. The pupil is now a detective trying to identify and correct answers (answers 4 and 5 are incorrect).

Wiliam (2017) offers this advice to teachers:

> I think the important point is firstly, you have to give students a completable task in order to take the feedback on board, and the second thing is you have to make them do it in front of you.

A teacher encouraging the learner to find and fix the error in front of them ensures the learner completes the task, otherwise the teacher can provide further feedback and guidance until they have answered the question correctly. By doing this the learner will have identified and hopefully understood where they went wrong.

In my experience, pupils often find this technique frustrating as they would simply prefer the teacher to tell them where they went wrong and how to fix it, or even better just tell them the correct answer! That would be an easier and quicker option, but the detective approach requires the learner to revisit their work, think hard and try to rectify their mistakes. We want pupils to be able to solve problems, not memorise solutions.

This approach works well in maths, but it can be used in a wide range of subjects. For example, if a pupil has incorrectly spelled a key word, the teacher can inform the pupil that a paragraph (or sentence) contains a spelling error they need to find and fix. The mistake could be literacy based or factual, but the same principle of finding and fixing the error applies.

This approach does require more time and effort from the pupil, but it is a clear example of feedback being 'more work for the recipient than the donor', as Wiliam and Leahy advised. This approach could also be used with peer assessment, with pupils helping one another to find and fix errors in their classwork.

Precise praise

Praise can be provided to pupils through written or verbal feedback. Verbal praise is often given to learners throughout a lesson; this can be reactive and responsive to something a pupil has said or done. Praise can be used to recognise when a pupil has achieved something or made progress and can motivate learners to keep going.

At times in my teaching career, I have felt unsure about how to approach praise. I have been encouraged to praise pupils more, but I have also been warned not to give praise excessively. I have been instructed not to praise basic expectations, but then advised to find opportunities to praise specific learners because they respond well to praise. It has been contrary and confusing.

Everyone likes to feel appreciated, whether in a personal or professional capacity. It is important to consider this with our pupils. It can be difficult when teaching a demanding timetable to notice the quiet child sitting at the back of the classroom who always listens carefully, follows instructions, meets deadlines and tries their best. Their efforts should not go unnoticed but should instead be recognised and appreciated. The same applies to all learners, with their efforts and progress being praised in some way.

Generic praise and comments such as 'great job' show appreciation but they do not provide any feedback to move learning forward. There can be a place in the classroom for those comments as a form of recognition, but meaningful feedback must be provided too.

A study published in 2023 by E. Schoneveld and E. Brummelman highlighted one of the potential problems with inflated praise in the classroom. The report explains:

> An experiment with primary school children showed that when children learned that another child received inflated praise (while an equally performing classmate received modest praise

> or no praise), they perceived this child as less smart but more hardworking. These studies provide converging evidence that teachers' inflated praise, although well-intentioned, can make children from low socioeconomic status backgrounds seem less smart, thereby reinforcing negative stereotypes about these children's academic abilities.

An earlier publication (Burnett, 2010), also focusing on praise in the primary classroom, addressed pupil preference in terms of the praise they receive. According to the study:

> Younger students prefer 'ability' feedback, and as they grow older their preference for 'effort' feedback increases. Most importantly, general, non-targeted praise was most commonly used in the classroom, but this type of praise is not effective because it is not linked to a specific behaviour or targeted to the successful completion of a task.

Praise, of course, is a form of feedback; it is important, but it must be genuine and appropriate. It should not be patronising, vague or given too lavishly. Author Doug Lemov writes about 'precise praise' in the classroom (2021). Lemov advises that when praise is given to pupils it should be clearly explained what they have done well at, instead of general comments such as 'well done, keep it up!' If the praise is precise, pupils have something concrete to be proud of that they can continue to do. This can also make the areas for improvement clearer to identify and understand. Precise praise is relevant to verbal and written feedback.

Lemov argues that praise shouldn't be given to students for meeting basic expectations, for example listening to the teacher, as this should be the norm in every lesson and can simply be acknowledged by the teacher. Praise should focus on behaviours not traits, i.e. things students can have control over and can act on and achieve. The teacher will use a range of factors to influence when, how and why praise is awarded in the classroom. As Lemov explains:

> Teachers ask questions every lesson, every day. Questioning can serve a range of purposes and functions in the classroom. Questioning is essential to check for understanding and elicit evidence of learning. Feedback is the flip side of questioning, as

the feedback provides confirmation of accuracy, can highlight gaps in knowledge and can lead to further elaboration.

The following case study considers four key questions linked to feedback to support teacher workload, planning and responsive teaching and ultimately to support pupil progress.

Case study: Enhancing feedback through questioning

Bio: David Vann is an experienced primary Year 6 teacher at Ferndown Middle School, Castleman Trust, Dorset.

For me, it all boils down to four key things to really improve the outcomes of my learners and improve my workload through the use of truly effective feedback. When I say improve, what I specifically mean is reduce, refine and make purposeful. I am sure for many other teachers out there that time is at an absolute premium. Faced with 30 or more children for five sessions a day (often ending up with 120 books to 'mark'), what I choose to do, within and after the lessons, must be meaningful and purposeful. All else, in my opinion, is a waste of time and serves no real purpose. If it's not helping my learners improve, why am I doing it?

1 Does everyone in the room know what you are learning? Are you sure?

For me, feedback starts right at the beginning, and is linked to the past. Does everyone know what they are learning and how to achieve that in small steps? Checking in here with shared understanding of the intention for the session, a worked example, sharing or creating the success criteria with the children and then re-exploring that with a critical lens is where the feedback starts. Misconceptions, misunderstandings and 'no understandings' all bubble to the surface, and as they rise feedback is immediate, refined and precise, targeted to one, some or all as appropriate. I have often thought (or assumed) my pupils knew things they were actually unable to recall.

2 What does it all mean though? Give me an example.

Sharing the vocabulary that we will be using in the lesson and asking for feedback on their understanding and familiarity with these terms has proven to be important for me. Critical really. If my learners do not have (or are unable to use) the vocabulary we will be using for the session, I may as well teach the lesson in a different language! Asking the learners for definitions in context, linking language to other situations or addressing real misunderstanding or knowledge gaps is an entry point to a lesson. 'Tell me what you understand this word to mean. Great, (or, oh my goodness)!' This requires meaningful and enabling feedback to individuals and then grants access to the lesson ahead. Don't underestimate the importance of this basic step; it's a gateway to either a highly productive session, or a chaotic, confused one. Oracy often means understanding.

3 What do you understand so far? Tell me. Be clear, be precise, be specific.

This is a slide that is used as a systematic and strategic provocation for the learners in the room. After an 'input', or a shared or worked example, or an 'I do, we do, you do', this is the slide that will never be left out of any of my lessons. We are 15 minutes in and I think I've done a solid job on explaining, modelling and involving learners. Then I ask what my students understand so far, and oh how wrong I was! This is a cold call, no opt out, partner-talk-question where all learners in the room *have* to generate an informed answer. The feedback is so targeted and precise here, as it responds directly to individual needs, immediately and at the point of learning. The session is being held tightly on course and pivots and adapts as those learners require.

4 Are they showing what I think they know?

Looking through books at the end of a session can be useful or it can be a complete waste of time, turning into an unnecessary administrative task. Marking is dead, long live feedback! Identifying specific improvements for the learner, not the work exclusively, based on the post-session feedback is really impactful. Clustering any common misconceptions to feed into next session's retrieval, whole class feedback for the next session, 'Last lesson I noticed... what did you understand when... look at this one, why is it incorrect/is it incorrect, and if so, why?' Or one-to-one sessions, small group intervention, with learners during the next session, or later the same day (if ever possible) directly addressing what was found and feeding back precisely, then seeing improvement and feeding back live.

'That's it, look at the difference now. Show me why this is now better or correct.' All the feedback in these examples is manipulated into key questions to use the 'data' from class books effectively and have an impact. This will avoid trawling through masses of books with 19 different coloured highlights and 176 different symbols that take hours to produce, and end up with a hand up and a statement, 'I don't get it...' What? You mean a coloured highlighter didn't unveil and explain the concept I failed to in the lesson? Surprising... Which leads us back to the first point and our initial questions.

So, to summarise: kill mindless, meaningless marking; only feedback on what matters; build understanding in small steps with constant feedback; use your learners' explanations as an instructional amplifier; check language access; check for understanding through precise dialogue; live feedback at the point of learning; and check – take feedback, then check again and pivot.

Oh, and you have 55 minutes – good luck!

Verbal feedback stamps

I have never used (and have never been asked or told to use) a verbal feedback stamp (VFS). However, I have seen plenty of these in action in different classrooms. The concept is simple: a teacher places a stamp in a class book to illustrate verbal feedback has been provided to the pupil.

Many educators believe that these stamps are a thing of the past, alongside ideas like 'thinking hats', 'learning styles' and the 'brain gym'. However, in 2023 Teacher Tapp asked the question to primary teachers, 'Are you expected to write or stamp VF or similar in books to indicate where you have given verbal feedback?'

From the total of 3,394 responses, the results were:

Yes – 47%

No – 47%

Not relevant – 6%

This result surprised many, but from my experiences working with schools in a consultancy role I was not shocked. I continue to see stamps, comments or a signature with a date written in class books to show verbal feedback has been provided. I have spoken to teachers about this and the majority of the responses indicate that they have no choice as they are instructed to by senior leaders due to school policy.

There are some teachers who argue that the stamp is a useful reminder to the teacher and pupil that dialogue has taken place, but the generic stamp or comment doesn't remind anyone what the feedback stated or focused on. It can be argued that the stamp is used to communicate to parents, line managers or external visitors (inspectors, for example) that feedback has taken place in a lesson.

Nikki McGee, a subject specialist lead for religion and philosophy, has reflected on how she and her colleagues used a VFS but later moved towards whole class feedback, without the need for the stamp.

> I used these at the time – my whole school did and those who thought they were awful kept quiet. We stamped and the student wrote next to it the feedback given. I wonder if this was a necessary step towards whole class feedback. We realised quite quickly that the stamp wasn't needed but it was a step for us in realising that feedback could be more than us writing in books. The stamps disappeared but the student kept recording our feedback, which then became a version of whole class feedback for us to refine. […] Often, the practices that we now reject may have been a necessary step to get us to where we are now. Thinking has moved on, but that could be because of the practice we now ridicule. It should

also prompt some humility and healthy scepticism about what we are currently doing.

The decision to implement something as part of a whole-school policy is often well intentioned. It has been argued that stamps such as a VFS support teacher workload, as it is quick and easy to stamp a book as opposed to writing comments in each. However, the stamp is a poor proxy to demonstrate feedback and learning. Just because a book has stamps, it does not mean that meaningful dialogue with feedback has taken place or that the pupil has made progress.

There are a few key questions to be raised about the use of the VFS.

- **What is the purpose of the VFS?**
- **Does the VFS make any difference or impact?**
- **Who is the VFS for?**

The answer to the first question is that the VFS only serves to tell someone outside of the classroom that a conversation has taken place between the pupil and teacher. This links with the second question, as the stamp itself doesn't provide any feedback or help to the learner. It can provide a visual reminder to the learner and teacher that dialogue has taken place, but it doesn't give any more information other than 'verbal feedback given', so it is a relatively weak reminder.

The third question illustrates that the VFS is simply used to keep a record and have evidence of feedback. This is likely to be for the benefit of school leaders, external visitors or parents. However, this record doesn't show what feedback was provided to the pupil or if they have acted on it. The only evidence of feedback should be the progress learners make as a result of feedback given to them and to which they have responded.

Verbal feedback is important and takes place every lesson, but recording this by pen or stamp is unnecessary, unhelpful and a waste of precious lesson and learning time. While there are some arguments for using a VFS, I and others across the profession view the stamps as a lethal mutation of verbal feedback. The research is clear that verbal feedback can have a positive impact on teacher workload and pupil progress. However, there is a lack of evidence to support or promote the use of verbal feedback stamps in schools.

Verbal feedback with recorded audio

It is not always possible to provide verbal feedback, and a verbal feedback conversation can only take place within a lesson (or the following lesson after the review of pupil work). However, there are a range of tech tools that enable teachers to record feedback and that audio feedback can be shared with pupils (and other teachers, leaders or parents).

A benefit of recorded feedback is that teachers can record verbal feedback outside of the lesson for their pupils to listen to. This can replace written comments with recorded audio. Learners can listen to the feedback in a lesson or outside of the classroom (in their home environment, for example). Another benefit of audio feedback is that the learner can listen to the feedback more than once, which may mean they are less likely to forget the feedback.

Audio feedback can support teacher workload, decreasing time spent marking and increasing time for other aspects of teacher planning, preparation and assessment. Audio feedback can encourage pupils to engage with the feedback provided, to support their learning. Examples of audio feedback include Vibbl.com and the Teacher Fast Feedback digital tool (find out more at www.teacherfastfeedback.com).

Special educational needs and disabilities

Every teacher is a teacher of special educational needs and disabilities (SEND) pupils, but as teachers know, individuals vary significantly in terms of the difficulties and challenges they face. The EEF Feedback Guidance Report (2021) states: 'To a great extent, good teaching for pupils with SEND is good teaching for all.'

Key principles about effective feedback can and should be applied to feedback given to SEND learners. Every pupil should be provided with feedback to help them make progress and every pupil should have access to feedback that is understandable, helpful and actionable. However, a barrier for learners with SEND can be understanding the feedback provided to them.

The EEF SEND guidance report suggests that 'small-group and one-to-one interventions can be a powerful tool but must be used carefully.' Where possible, one-to-one feedback conversations can help learners with SEND to use and act on the feedback they have received.

Feedback can be linked to the following, based on where teaching takes place in the UK.

- Individual Education Plan (IEP) or Education, Health and Care (EHC) plan in England.
- Individual Development Plan (IDP) in Wales.
- Statement of Special Educational Needs (SEN) in Northern Ireland.
- Co-ordinated Support Plan (CSP) in Scotland.

These documents are designed to focus on individual needs and targets, as well as offering the classroom teacher further insight and guidance. Training should be offered to teachers, with explanations and advice on how to use the information provided to help with lesson planning, design, delivery and feedback.

Karen Wespieser, educator and writer, has highlighted a problem for teachers to be aware of (2021). Wespieser argues:

> If much of the evidence base in education is still half-baked, the evidence base in SEND is raw. Despite the medical nature of some SEND there is limited robust evidence on how best to support these learners educationally.

Further research is required to ensure that learners with SEND are represented and to further help teachers support individuals in their classes. As covered in the introduction to this book, evidence alone shouldn't guide teaching and learning principles and policy. As a profession, we can draw on the experience and expertise of those around us, which is certainly the case with experts in the field of SEND.

The following case study is written by Amjad Ali, a specialist in the field of SEND. Ali offers advice and guidance for all teachers with a focus on providing feedback to pupils with SEND.

Case study: Feedback and learners with SEND

Bio: Amjad Ali is an experienced classroom teacher, senior leader and author of *A little guide for teachers: Special Educational Needs* (2024). You can find out more about Amjad and check out his teaching and learning resources via his website www.TryThisTeaching.com/about. He is active on X @TeachLeadAAl and Instagram @TryThisTeaching.

As educators, the responsibility to provide meaningful feedback to students is vital. However, when students have SEND this task can become even more crucial and nuanced. This case study examines the strategies and considerations for teachers in giving effective feedback to students with SEND.

Background

Meet Zakariya, an English teacher in a bustling secondary school with a diverse student profile. In his class he has Sammi, a bright and enthusiastic student with dyslexia. Sammi is eager to learn, but he often struggles with spelling and organising his thoughts cohesively in writing assignments.

Challenges faced

Zakariya faces the issue of balancing the need to challenge Sammi academically while providing feedback that supports his learning process. Traditional methods of feedback, such as long written comments in books or text, might not be as effective for Sammi due to his dyslexia. Additionally, the fear of discouraging Sammi or damaging his confidence looms large.

Strategies implemented

1 Vary modes of feedback

Understanding that written feedback might not be the most effective for Sammi, Zakariya explores alternative modalities.

He starts recording verbal feedback on Sammi's assignments using voice notes (apps and online tools are available for this now). This not only provides a more personalised touch but also allows Sammi to listen to the feedback repeatedly, aiding his understanding.

2 Clear and specific feedback

Instead of generic comments, Zakariya ensures his feedback is clear, specific and actionable. For instance, instead of saying 'good job', he might say, 'I like how you used descriptive language in this paragraph to paint a vivid picture. Let's work on organising your ideas in the next draft.'

3 Peer support and collaborative learning

Zakariya incorporates peer review sessions into his lessons, pairing Sammi with a supportive classmate like Isaac, for example. This not only helps in improving Sammi's work through peer feedback but also fosters a sense of collaboration and community within the class.

4 Visual aids and mind mapping

Knowing that visual aids can be beneficial for students with dyslexia, Zakariya introduces mind mapping techniques. Before starting a writing assignment, he encourages Sammi to create a visual outline of his ideas. This helps him in organising his thoughts before putting pen to paper.

5 Regular check-ins and goal setting

Zakariya schedules regular one-on-one check-ins with Sammi to discuss his progress. During these meetings, they set achievable goals together. This empowers Sammi to take ownership of his learning while providing Zakariya with insights into his challenges and strengths.

Results and observations

Over the course of the term, Zakariya notices improvements in Sammi's writing and overall confidence. His assignments show better organisation, improved spelling (thanks to assistive technology) and a deeper engagement with the subject matter.

Moreover, Sammi's enthusiasm for learning English has grown. He actively participates in class discussions, feeling more secure in expressing his ideas. Zakariya also observes a positive change in Sammi's demeanour – he is more willing to take risks in his writing, knowing that his teacher values his efforts.

Reflections and next steps

Reflecting on this experience, Zakariya realises the importance of individualised approaches to feedback for students with SEND. What works for one student might not work for another, emphasising the need for flexibility and creativity in teaching practices.

Moving forward, Zakariya plans to continue refining his feedback strategies for students with diverse needs. He seeks to collaborate more closely with the school's special educational needs co-ordinator, drawing on their expertise to create an even more inclusive learning environment.

In the journey of educating students with SEND, the role of feedback cannot be overstated. It serves not only as a tool for academic growth but also as a means to nurture confidence and a love for learning. By tailoring feedback to meet the unique needs of students like Sammi, educators can truly make a difference in their educational journey.

Through Zakariya's example, teachers can glean valuable insights into the art of providing effective feedback to students with SEND, paving the way for a more inclusive and empowering classroom environment.

English as an additional language

I spent five years teaching in an international school context, from 2016 to 2021. The schools followed the UK curriculum, but the pupils were diverse, with a vast range of different nationalities represented. Supporting pupils with English as an additional language (EAL) was an essential part of my lesson planning. Ensuring EAL learners understood the feedback (from the teacher, their peers and when delivered to the whole class) was paramount. Through verbal feedback I was able to communicate clearly, speak slowly when necessary and check for understanding.

I can recall a conversation with a very hardworking and conscientious EAL pupil. The feedback I provided was focusing on literacy, and the pupil let out a big sigh and showed a look of disappointment. I asked what was wrong and she told me that she felt like every teacher, every lesson, every day was always telling her to work on and improve her literacy and English skills. She found this difficult and demoralising because English wasn't her first language, and she didn't have many opportunities to speak English at home.

This conversation was honest and important because it helped me to understand the frustrations felt by my pupil. To be able to communicate in more than one language is admirable; it should be celebrated. But with constant feedback focusing on literacy and language, for my pupil sadly it was disheartening.

To be able to understand, process and recall information in a second language requires a lot of concentration, effort and skill. An article published by REAL Learners highlighted this point, stating:

> Feedback can only be effective if children understand it. Pupils learning EAL are not only learning English, but also having to process a massive range of cognitive and academic processes through this unfamiliar language. How do you find and correct your own mistakes if you are unfamiliar with the language those mistakes occur in?

Valid points are raised about the use of peer assessment and self-assessment with EAL pupils. EAL pupils may lack confidence, skills or the ability to provide meaningful feedback to their peers. How can teachers support EAL pupils with peer feedback, which involves providing it to their peers and receiving it too?

Self-assessment can be challenging, especially for EAL pupils. How can teachers support pupils with self-assessment? Chapter 4 focuses on strategies to support self-assessment, with examples and resources that are appropriate for pupils with EAL. Technology, when used carefully and purposefully, can support EAL pupils with the feedback they receive, either through the use of audio feedback to listen to or translation and vocabulary tools.

The case study below offers further advice and insight about providing feedback to learners with EAL.

Case study: Providing feedback to learners with EAL

Bio: Beth Southern is an experienced EAL consultant and school leader who works closely with many schools across the UK and internationally, improving EAL provision and the experience for EAL learners every year. Beth is the founder of the EAL Hub, SEN Hub and EAL STAR, an assessment platform. You can follow Beth on X @Bethan_Southern.

There has been a lot of research surrounding the importance of feeding back to learners in schools, but what about when a child is new to English? How does that impact the giving of feedback?

Written marking policies are generally designed for native English speakers; they are not designed for a child who is learning content and language at the same time. Feedback can only be effective and informative if children understand what you are saying. Those who have EAL are learning brand new academic content, and at the same time they're learning the constructs of a new language (word order, grammar, syntax and vocabulary) – is it possible to find and correct your mistakes if you don't know they're mistakes yet, because the language is new?

For feedback to be effective, the process must be cyclical. This starts with the learner receiving feedback and engaging with it. The learner then modifies their understanding and applies what they have learned, ultimately improving their outcome. The process then begins again. But what do we need to consider when it comes to *how* we offer feedback and how we get learners to engage with it?

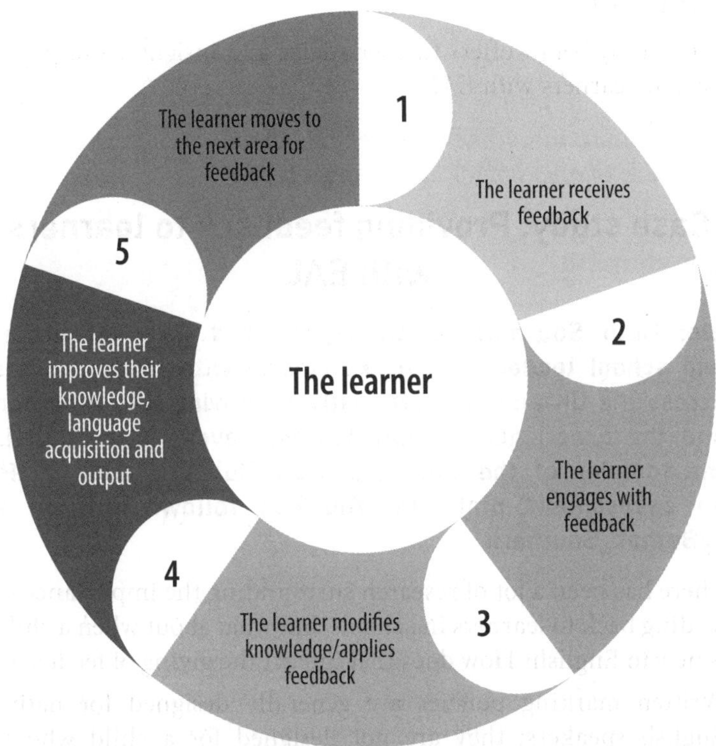

Maslow's hierarchy of needs

As with all learners, EAL students must have certain needs met before they can learn and engage with feedback. Maslow's 'hierarchy of needs' suggests that basic needs (physiological) need to be met and people need to feel safe before any learning can take place. With students that have recently arrived in the country, we often need to think about nurture first. This should focus on building their confidence and relationships so they can move towards the hierarchy level of 'belonging'. Before this level is reached, the students cannot learn regardless of how much scaffolding or feedback we put in place.

Once they have reached the belonging level they are in a good position to learn with support. With students who are new to English or new to the country, often a smile, positive affirmation, a sticker or a star works well. It is also possible to introduce visual feedback using symbols; this can help remove barriers to understanding when children are new to English. Children are more likely to feel valued, engaged in the lesson and part of the school community when they feel they have access to what is going on.

Questioning

When considering questioning techniques as a form of summative assessment, it is important to build in wait time. The average question is asked and answered in a classroom fairly quickly; this often does not provide enough time for an EAL learner to switch between languages and formulate an answer. As teachers we often pose questions, students respond, and the teacher evaluates – Dylan Wiliams calls this 'serial table tennis'.

It is a better approach to allow for more conversation between students, which involves posing a question, allowing thinking time and then asking for an answer or part answer before moving that answer around the room, thus allowing other students to add more or offer something different. Answers can be offered via speaking, drawing on a whiteboard or writing a single word or idea. This approach helps you as a teacher to see what learners know and it allows students more thinking time and the understanding that they don't need to offer a full answer, which removes some of the pressure associated with 'cold calling' (questioning that involves the teacher selecting a student to answer, instead of relying on volunteers). Focus on one method ('pose, pause, pounce, bounce', for example) so the students get used to it. It is then easy to implement and often leads to a greater depth of response and a wider pool of respondents.

Focus on what matters most

Hartshorn and Evans (2015) explain that written corrective feedback can either be focused (only selected error types are targeted) or comprehensive (most of the errors occurring in a student's piece of writing are targeted). Truscott (2020) argues that correcting comprehensively had 'no demonstrable gains' on language acquisition for EAL learners.

I would argue that it can be demoralising for an EAL learner to see every mistake highlighted in their work, as the chances are they will have made quite a lot of errors given that they are learning both content and language simultaneously. As such, try not to focus on every grammatical error. While it can be difficult to ignore glaring errors, it is important to sometimes look past these and consider structure, presentation, word choice, pronunciation and confidence in speaking. Finding ways to give feedback on areas of positivity can boost the motivation and confidence of learners. This then allows you to focus your corrections on key areas that are more manageable for the learner to improve upon. Using marking codes can provide direct correction, as opposed to simply highlighting or underlining errors, which is known as indirect correction. Indirect correction can leave learners unsure of how to make improvements, particularly when they are new to English.

Marking codes

For more proficient EAL learners, marking codes can be used effectively as a visual way of enabling the student more opportunities to correct their own work via direct and focused corrective feedback. Teachers use codes such as 'SP' for spelling, 'WO' for word order, 'EV' for evidence and 'VT' for verb tense. The key is using the codes consistently so that students can understand them and learn how to improve their work using the codes as a guide. Students need to be provided with scaffolded support in this process to begin with and should be offered clear explanations and examples of the different codes and how to make those changes. EAL students often find it easier to understand the codes rather than receiving longer written or verbal feedback, but the codes offer more than just providing them with ticks and crosses or highlighted errors, which don't assist them with trying to reflect and work independently to improve.

The use of marking codes should only be used for more proficient EAL learners as it is important to consider how a student corrects an error when they haven't fully learned how to apply the language being used. Using it alongside peer marking (ideally involving a native- or fluent-speaking student) can be useful as the peer can offer advice and guidance to help the EAL learner talk through the sentence to discuss possible changes or improvements. This consistent, interactive and supportive approach will help the EAL student to avoid the same mistakes moving forward.

Checklists for more advanced learners

Offering an EAL learner a checklist of what you are looking for can be a good way to help them improve their work. Similar to direct correction and marking codes, a checklist removes the pressure of not understanding what is wrong as they can be given a list with corresponding examples. Checklists make a functional bridge between learners' needs and their independent practice as they can be used as a safeguard against errors, making simple mistakes or skipping steps and information. Feedback can be focused on the checklist so teachers can point out where key things have not been achieved, thus streamlining feedback into manageable chunks.

Mistakes versus errors

When it comes to EAL learners it is important to know the difference between a mistake (something one-off that happened due to rushing, for example) and an error (something that happened because the student does not yet understand fully). Sometimes you can discover this information through questioning, asking them to write a simple sentence or asking them to tell you something using the specific skill you are focusing on. This helps you to assess what they know, rather than what was merely a mistake. Mistakes can be corrected via things such as marking codes, whereas errors require thorough teaching to help students understand why they got it wrong.

Ensure targets are achievable – cultural pressure to succeed

Work ethics and the pressure to achieve educational success vary across different cultures, so it is important to understand the culture of your learners so you can ensure that the way you give feedback is understandable. Similarly, the targets that you set need to be achievable for the student in relation to their academic ability and their language proficiency. It is important to avoid the possibility of learners being demoralised, 'losing face' or feeling like they have let their family down. These 'failure' mentalities are prevalent in cultures where a great deal of onus is placed on academic achievement, so as teachers it is vital that we give feedback and set targets carefully and according to individual student needs.

Conclusion

There is no one-size-fits-all solution when it comes to offering feedback to EAL learners. Many of the choices you make will be dependent on the student – how long they have been in school, how proficient they are in English and how much pressure they have from home to succeed academically. Feedback needs to be personalised, but it also needs to be consistent. Consistent methods allow the EAL learner to understand what is expected of them, for example using marking codes or specific questioning techniques. Feedback that is interactive and facilitates a student receiving, engaging with and acting upon with little time between is the most effective method because it allows for immediate reflection. Adding in support from peers or support staff can enable further discussion and sharing of good examples to assist EAL learners further. Finally, we must appreciate the importance of praise. Positive reinforcement of effort is hugely motivating in the classroom, helping us to overcome one of the greatest hurdles we face when working with EAL learners.

Verbal feedback and the 'curse of knowledge'

It is useful for teachers to be aware of the 'curse of knowledge' when providing feedback to pupils. The phrase was coined in 1989 by economists Camerer, Lowenstein and Weber, and the idea refers to a cognitive bias where individuals assume other people know what they know. This can include knowledge and understanding of key terms, concepts or background information that a person assumes others have.

Authors Chip and Dan Heath (2007) explain:

> Once we know something, we find it hard to imagine what it was like not to know it. Our knowledge has 'cursed' us. And it becomes difficult for us to share our knowledge with others, because we can't readily re-create our listeners' state of mind.

The bias of knowledge can make it difficult for experts to explain and teach content or concepts to novices, and can therefore present a challenge within teaching and learning. This is an unusual paradox for teachers, as the greater their expertise and subject knowledge, the more difficult it can be to explain to learners. This is something teachers should be mindful of when planning, designing and delivering lessons. The curse of knowledge can create issues with communication and ultimately become a barrier to effective teaching and learning, especially regarding feedback.

There are some ways that teachers can avoid succumbing to the curse of knowledge in the classroom. It is important to be patient with pupils. It can be frustrating for a teacher when pupils are struggling to grasp a concept or content that the teacher knows well and has repeated many times. Patience, empathy and understanding are all important, especially as mixed-attainment classes will often contain pupils that learn and progress at different levels and paces. Learning is difficult, and every expert was once a novice – it can be easy for an expert to forget that!

Instead of assuming pupils have prior knowledge and understanding of the content discussed, it is essential to check first or provide an explanation or reminder for learners. Pupils with EAL or SEND may not possess the vocabulary to access the lesson content or understand the feedback provided to them, but if the teacher is aware of this they can give support to make the lesson content and feedback accessible and understandable. The teacher should not move on to the next topic without thoroughly checking for understanding and accuracy.

Pupils may ask a teacher for clarification if they do not understand or follow the content, but this does not always happen. A pupil could be reluctant to ask the teacher, especially if their peers seem to possess the knowledge and understanding they don't, as they may lack the confidence or worry the knowledge deficit is their fault. Encouraging pupils to give feedback about their understanding and ensuring a safe and positive learning environment can help to challenge the curse of knowledge.

A teacher cannot revisit every aspect of the lesson material – there simply isn't enough time and learners will have prior knowledge they can build upon – so it can be difficult for the teacher to know whether or not certain content should be revisited. This is why using feedback to support lesson planning and responsive teaching is so important.

If there is doubt about pupils possessing the required prior knowledge and understanding, double check or provide further support and explanation. This is an essential part of the feedback loop, where pupils demonstrate evidence of performance or learning and the teacher provides feedback that the pupils then act upon to move forward and close any knowledge gaps.

Chapter summary

- There are many benefits to using verbal feedback in the lesson to support individuals or communicate to the whole class.
- There are efficient methods that can be carried out in the lesson, such as the detective strategy and precise praise.
- Teachers should be continually aware of the limitations of working memory and the impact this can have on forgetting verbal feedback if it is not processed and acted upon.
- Younger children and pupils with SEND or EAL can all benefit greatly from feedback conversations in the lesson, as can all learners.
- There are digital tools available to support the recording of audio feedback that pupils can access inside and outside of a lesson.
- The key principles of effective feedback apply to verbal feedback: learners should understand it and it should be helpful and actionable.

Chapter 3
Whole class feedback

The purpose of the whole class feedback (WCF) concept is to ensure meaningful feedback is provided to all pupils while being communicated in a way that is sustainable and workload friendly for teachers. WCF has understandably gained a lot of interest in recent years among teachers and school leaders. The Michaela Community School in Wembley, London have led the way, inspiring other schools to move away from traditional and time-consuming methods of marking and towards the 'Michaela way' of WCF.

Although this approach has grown in popularity, there are many schools that are yet to adopt WCF or are reluctant to do so. There are misconceptions about WCF, for example that it ignores individual learners' needs and lacks support for pupils. If carried out effectively, WCF can help individuals to make progress – it is not just an approach to reduce teacher workload.

If WCF is already in use, among other strategies, to provide feedback to your pupils, then this chapter aims to provide practical tips and advice to ensure WCF feedback is efficient and effective. If there is uncertainty or reluctance to embrace WCF, this chapter will provide some insight and inspiration.

A point about WCF that teachers should be aware of is that learners may assume feedback delivered to the whole class is not relevant to them and therefore may not engage with it. This was illustrated by John Hattie (2011):

> Most teacher feedback is presented to groups and so often students believe that such class feedback is not about them – hence the dissipation of provided feedback.

It is important to explain to pupils that while WCF may seem generalised, it is intended to support all individuals in the classroom. Any feedback presented to the class, either verbally, written or via technology, should be designed to help all learners progress, although they may be at different stages in the learning process or have different levels of knowledge, understanding and recall.

Further research is required into WCF, but there is a lot of enthusiasm about this approach from teachers, as demonstrated in the case studies throughout this chapter. The case studies include examples from primary and secondary schools, across different subjects. Key principles linked to effective feedback, such as focusing on improving the pupil and not just the work, while being understandable, helpful and actionable, also apply to WCF.

There are different ways in which teachers can provide WCF. It can be provided as part of live feedback in the lesson or when pupils are working on a set task that is circulated around the classroom. While this is taking place the teacher can give individual feedback to learners, verbally or through short written comments or marking codes, but if the teacher notices a trend of errors or some general mistakes or misconceptions the lesson can be stopped to address them. WCF lends itself well to responsive teaching.

WCF can support the whole class to further understand a concept, spell words correctly or tackle a problem accurately. This is clearly nothing new and is quite simply good teaching; however, WCF often hasn't received the credit it deserves as a method of providing feedback to learners.

Pre-emptive feedback

In terms of our health, prevention is better than a cure – this is the argument behind vaccines and the importance of leading a healthy lifestyle. It is of course far better to prevent an illness in the first place than attempt to cure one. We can apply this philosophy to the classroom – teachers can anticipate the mistakes pupils will make in the classroom, meaning they can intervene before those mistakes are made.

I have taught Year 7 history for over a decade, and the unit focusing on the events of 1066 has always been the first unit studied on the curriculum. Every year there are pupils who misspell the words 'soldier' and 'heir'. Another mistake that students typically make in this unit is confusing the key individuals and contenders to the throne, Harald Hardrada and Harold Godwinson.

Instead of allowing another year group to make these mistakes, I made sure that I clearly and thoroughly explained the differences between Harald Hardrada and Harold Godwinson. I found and planned ways to support my pupils to help them understand and recall the distinction between the two important figures. I also ensured key words such as 'soldier' and 'heir' were visible to support the pupils in spelling the terms correctly. By doing these things, if pupils listened to and acted on my advice and pre-emptive feedback, I no longer had to provide feedback about spelling 'soldier' accurately or explain yet again the differences between Harald Hardrada and Harold Godwinson.

As teachers gain experience, they become familiar with commonly occurring misconceptions and mistakes. Instead of repeating the same feedback year after year across different classes, teachers can prevent pupils from making common mistakes before their work is submitted.

Daisy Christodoulou (2018) addresses this, writing:

> Lots of students make similar mistakes to other people in the class and to people who have done the task before, so in a lot of cases you can anticipate the kinds of feedback you should be giving. You can deal with lots of things at once, so I think the way for a teacher to cut down on their workload is to start to anticipate what's going to be a typical response and how they're going to respond to that.

The 'prevention is better than a cure' concept with pre-emptive feedback means that, as teachers, we are using previous feedback to ensure pupils don't repeat those mistakes and the same feedback doesn't need to be repeated. There are lots of ways this can be achieved in the classroom; one method that can help pupils to consistently spell complex or difficult words correctly is to provide them with a literacy word mat. Pupils should be encouraged to double check spellings of key words as they are completing tasks and once more before they submit their classwork.

A word mat can contain all the key words from a unit, as shown in the following primary example.

Planets

Mercury
Venus
Earth
Mars
Jupiter
Saturn
Uranus
Neptune

Earth and space

Vocabulary

Astronaut – A person who is trained to travel in a spacecraft.

Atmosphere – The gases held by gravity around Earth and other planets.

Planet – Large natural objects that orbit or travel around stars.

Constellations – A group of stars in the sky.

Galaxy – A collection of between thousands and billions of stars held together by gravity.

Orbit – The curved path that a planet, satellite or spacecraft moves as it circles around another object.

There are lots of other ways in which the word mats can be used in a lesson, for example during paired quizzing. Pupils can work together in pairs and ask their partner to spell a key term correctly, or they could take it in turns to pick a word from the mat and tell their partner its meaning and what they recall about the term.

Word mats can be used at home with parents to support spellings or for retrieval practice quizzing. Alternatively, a 'knowledge organiser' (a document containing the key information from a topic, see page 164) can be used inside and outside of the classroom for the same purposes. Knowledge organisers can include factual content and concepts.

Question banks and misconception banks

Across a department, whether that be a year group, key stage or subject, there should be a consistent set of questions (and answers) focusing on the specified knowledge that forms the curriculum. These question banks can be used at different points in the learning process to check for understanding or help long-term learning with recall.

Question banks can be completed as a department, or individuals can be tasked with creating question banks for particular year groups or topics, which can then be shared and used collectively. A question bank is a shared set of questions that all pupils are asked and are expected to answer, for either formative or summative assessment purposes.

Question banks stored in a shared space can support teacher workload and ensure consistency. Teachers can decide how they ask the questions in the classroom, such as by means of mini whiteboards or an online quizzing tool. Teachers can exercise their professional judgement and autonomy when it comes to their preferred style of quizzing, but the questions asked across different classes should be the same. This approach promotes quality assurance and can lead to discussion and reflection on careful question design.

Question banks should be made available in a shared space for teachers to access and use in their lessons, for example using an online drive or folder. Once question banks are created, they can be reviewed and adapted on a regular basis. Linked to this concept are 'misconception banks', where common misconceptions or general mistakes can be collated and recorded.

NQTs and ECTs might not be aware of the mistakes and misconceptions that arise, so it is a good idea to discuss this issue and provide support at a departmental level. It is highly likely the same errors are being made across different classes, so a record should be kept (such as a bank of misconceptions for a specific unit, topic or concept) for inexperienced teachers to discuss, reflect on and prepare for when planning lessons.

Teachers and departments should consider the following key questions.

- **What are the common misconceptions that occur in this topic or lesson?**
- **How can I identify and address these misconceptions with my class?**
- **What key terms are often challenging to spell?**
- **What other literacy errors are common with this topic or task?**

Creating a bank of misconceptions and mistakes can be useful to support other colleagues and prepare future planning. A misconception bank could also be created with the purpose of sharing and discussing with learners, and it can be a document they can refer and have access to. The following is an example of a misconception bank to support the teaching of a unit at GCSE level.

GCSE history: Misconceptions bank
Germany 1918–1933

- The Nazi party was founded by Anton Drexler, not Adolf Hitler. Pupils often refer to Hitler as the founder of the Nazi party but this is untrue – he was actually the 55th member to join.
- Some pupils do not realise that the Nazis did not start WW1; the party was not established until after WW1 in 1919.
- Hitler was not German; he was born in Austria (German speaking). This surprises a lot of pupils.
- The Nazis did not invent anti-Semitism. There are examples of hostility towards and abusive treatment of the Jews throughout history It is worth explaining this to pupils for context.
- Other minorities were targeted by the Nazi party. Examples of these should be explored in addition to treatment of the Jewish people.
- Pupils have a belief that the Nazi party was always considered evil and was hated. Although they did receive opposition, the party certainly had a lot of support and momentum with the rise of extremism.
- Hitler was not the President of Germany in 1933 – Hindenburg was. After the death of Hindenburg in 1934, Hitler consolidated his power as Führer.

Director of education at Steplab and author Peps Mccrea writes about 'flipping failure' when it comes to mistakes and misconceptions. Through his weekly email, Mccrea (2023) gives advice to teachers:

> Flipping failure is about reducing the negative impact of mistakes and misconceptions before and when they arise and helping students to ultimately view them as an opportunity to be embraced, rather than an experience to be avoided. [...] One of the most powerful ways we can flip failure is by constantly being on the lookout for when students make mistakes or misconceptions, and when that happens, taking the opportunity to highlight them, analyse them, and ensure that everyone (not just the person who made them) learns from them.

According to Mccrea, there are three ways in which teachers can flip failure in the classroom with mistakes and misconceptions. The first is by pre-emptively communicating how failure is a normal part of life and the learning process. Secondly, teachers can reframe and celebrate failure as an opportunity to learn, and the third way is to focus on the mistake rather than the mistake maker.

Modelling

Modelling can serve a range of different purposes, including acting as pre-emptive feedback. As Hendrick and Macpherson (2017) point out, 'It's very difficult to be excellent if you don't know what excellence looks like.'

The following example is taken from my classroom, when I was teaching Year 7 very early in the academic year. After pupils had submitted their work, I noticed the majority of responses were accurate but lacked detail and supporting explanations. Instead of writing 'add more detail' on most of the pupils' work, I combined whole class feedback and modelling.

In the next lesson I informed the class that their answers were accurate. This was very pleasing for me to see as it demonstrated a correct understanding of the subject content. However, I explained to the class that I expected written responses to include more supporting detail. I realised my pupils would understand what 'add more detail' meant, but they may not have known what that looked like or how to add more detail to their answers. To help them grasp this, I showed the class a common response: 'Three men wanted to become King in 1066.'

This statement is correct (although there were four potential contenders to the throne, but we had not yet discussed Edgar the Atheling), but it doesn't demonstrate knowledge of why there was a succession crisis in 1066. The sentence does not explain who the three contenders to the throne were, nor does it provide any further information about their background and significance.

I then provided the class with the following, more detailed response. We read this together, and I was able to show how to add more detail to the initial basic response.

> In January 1066 King Edward the Confessor died, which caused many issues as he did not have a son or direct heir to the throne. There were three main contenders to the throne. The first contender was Harold Godwinson, a powerful and wealthy nobleman with a large army who owned a lot of land across the country. Harold Godwinson was related to Edward through marriage. Harald Hardrada was another contender keen to seize the English throne. Harald Hardrada was a Viking and King

> of Norway. Although his claim to the throne was weak, he was a distant relative of King Cnut, and he was previously King of England. Finally, the third contender to the throne was William, Duke of Normandy. Although he was not an Englishman, he was a distant relative of Edward and claimed Edward had promised him the throne in 1051.

Through the use of questioning, the class explored and discussed how further detail could be added to this answer, for example by specifically elaborating on key points such as explaining how Harold Godwinson and Edward were related through marriage. As a class we discussed literacy elements, for example the structure and use of different paragraphs to write about the different contenders to the throne. This task was designed to help learners understand how to add supporting detail so they could then use this skill and their knowledge to do so in the future, hence improving the learner, not just the piece of work.

Pupils then revisited their written work and were tasked with selecting three basic sentences to rewrite, with a focus on adding more historical supporting detail. Once pupils could understand what 'more detail' looked like, they could attempt to improve their work through elaboration and extension.

The example task could be provided to the class as a retrieval practice opportunity. For example, a basic statement can be on display on the board and learners have to elaborate on the original point, extending with additional information they can recall from long-term memory. Alternatively, this could be used as a DIRT task (dedicated improvement and reflection time) where pupils act on a section of their work selected by the teacher (or possibly through peer or self-assessment) and develop the points further. If it is not designed to be a retrieval task, then pupils could refer back to their class notes, knowledge organiser, class book or textbook to help them add further information.

Visualisers

One staple piece of classroom equipment for many teachers is the visualiser. The visualiser is not new, and it isn't technical or complex – previously teachers used an overhead projector in a similar manner to support pupils. A visualiser is a digital camera that can reflect images onto the screen in your classroom.

If your school has access to tablet devices, it may be possible to use a mirroring function to project an image on the tablet onto the screen. The visualiser is a simple and versatile device that can have multiple uses in the classroom; it can be used for modelling, reading through answers, importing and drafting and providing WCF.

The following case study by geography teacher Sarah Larsen explores the use of a visualiser in the classroom to provide feedback in a way that supports teachers' workloads and pupils' progress.

Case study: Visualisers in the classroom

Bio: Sarah Larsen is an experienced secondary geography teacher and a link tutor for a school-centred teacher training initiative. She is active on X @sarahlarsen74 and you can read her blog at https://sarahlarsen.school.blog/

My visualiser has become my absolute prized possession! I cannot remember how I ever used to teach without it, from using it to demonstrate how to use grid references, to live marking a student's piece of work so that the rest of the class can think about how to improve theirs. It is the one piece of classroom equipment I could never be without.

The following is a step-by-step account of how I use the visualiser to provide the first part of a model GCSE answer to guide my Year 10 students so they could successfully complete their own answers. On reflection I was very pleased with various aspects of this task, not least the quality of work produced by the students at the end of the exercise.

Step-by-step account

I display an exam question on the board and the students swiftly write it in their class books, including how many marks it is worth for future reference. The question is: 'Explain the causes of desertification.' [6 marks]

I explain to the students that they are going to use their knowledge from previous lessons to attempt this question and that I am going to talk them through the first part of the model answer. This is a mixed-attainment class, but as I frequently tell them, I teach everybody how to get a grade 9.

I tell the class that for the next few minutes I expect their undivided attention, and that all of their eyes should be on the screen so they can view my writing projected by the visualiser. I instruct my class to listen, not to write anything or speak unless I ask them to. Impeccable behaviour is paramount if all students are to benefit from this.

I sit down at my visualiser with a copy of the question on a piece of paper. I tell the class I am going to 'think out loud' to model how they should approach the question. I circle the command word 'explain', and I cold call a student to remind the class what the difference is between this word and the command word 'describe'. I use 'pose, pause, pounce, bounce' as the style of questioning so that all students have to think before somebody is chosen to answer. If the first student doesn't know I will move on to another, but I will always return to the original student and ask them to give me the correct answer.

I also circle the number of marks available and select another student to ask them to remind us how many developed points need to be made (two) and what the vital elements are (include an example of a place where desertification is occurring, and key terms must also be used along with the development of key points).

I begin the answer on paper under the visualiser. I start by writing a sentence to define desertification, and I tell the class I am doing this to show the examiner that I understand what it means. I then write a second sentence to state one reason for desertification (there are a number of factors I could use – I choose to write about over-cultivation due to population pressure). I also state an example of where in the world this is happening (the Sahel region, Africa).

I put my pen down and request feedback from the class. I ask a student whether they think I have written enough for my first developed point. Correctly, they tell me that I haven't – I ask them why. They tell me that I need to explain how this factor is contributing to desertification. Correct.

I add another sentence to state what is happening in the Sahel region regarding over-cultivation – in essence, growing populations leading to more crops being grown repeatedly on soils that are not left to recover.

I put my pen down and ask another student if this has been fully explained. Have I linked it back to the question and have I made it explicitly clear how over-cultivation causes desertification? The class is unsure. I read back my initial answer. I then ask the class, does my answer tell the whole story? Is there anything more I need to say? After questioning a few more students, the class agree that I have not told the whole story.

I add another sentence to explain that by not leaving the land to recover, fertility of the soil decreases, which stops crops or natural vegetation from growing, leading to exposure of the soil and soil erosion, meaning that no vegetation can grow again, which leads to desertification. Once again, I put my pen down and ask another student if this answer is sufficient. The student takes a few seconds to read it. The student tells me they think I have written enough for my first developed point, so I ask the student to tell me why. They answer that they can see I have described the whole process from start to finish, and that I have linked the answer back to the question.

I also point out that I have included a range of key terms in my answer, and I circle each of them to make them clear to the class. I remind the class that the answer is not finished as a second developed point is required to achieve full marks. I tell the class that I am not going to complete this answer as I want them to think about how to do this in the same way they watched me complete the first section.

I remove the image of my answer from the visualiser and give the students eight minutes to complete a full answer of their own, thinking about what they have just seen me do. Usually in the exam they would have six minutes as it tends to be one minute per mark, but as they are still practising I am giving them slightly longer, though I still want them to answer in timed conditions.

I provide a sentence starter on the written board to support students who are struggling and help get them started with their answer. I circulate around the room while they are working to assist with any queries or difficulty getting started. I make sure I check in with students I am aware tend to struggle; I do so early on to ensure they are happy, and I encourage those who aren't to tell me verbally what they think they should write first.

I remind other students who claim they have finished that they still need to develop their first point further as they have not told the full story, and I remind students to use specific phrases, such as 'this means that…'

After the time is up, I ask a student who has made a good attempt (although still with room for improvement) if I can place their work under the visualiser for the class to see. I only ever do this with their consent. I then live mark their piece of work, inviting other students to tell me what they have done well and what needs improving. As the students provide feedback I annotate around the answer for the class to see. I give the response a final mark and explain why it would get this mark (in this specific example, the student achieved 5 out 6 as their first point wasn't developed sufficiently).

I return the answer to the student so they can act on the feedback and improve their response. I freeze the board so the class can still see the feedback and I provide the class with some time to improve their answer based on the feedback they observed me giving to the student under the visualiser spotlight.

Reflection

This exercise took approximately 25 minutes, which was half of the lesson. In previous years I would have set the students off on this task by simply reminding them of the content of the answer, with perhaps a few key terms on the board as a prompt.

I would have taken their class books in two weeks later, marked them and laboriously written the same comments several times in many students' books. By the time they received the feedback it would be so long after the event that they had very likely forgotten what the question was about and what their thought processes were at the time, and there was a high chance they would not have understood the written comments I had spent a significant amount of time writing out in each book.

Until a few years ago students wouldn't have been given any time to improve their answers! No one moved forward and the same mistakes would have been made again the next time students practised an exam question.

Combining the use of a visualiser with immediate feedback and modelling has meant that my students now know far better how to approach an exam question, and improvements can be made in the moment. Through asking students questions about my written response, I make them think hard, a vital step that contributes to the required change in long-term memory, which they will have to rely on in the final exam.

I was pleased with the student's responses and outcomes and their willingness to enter into an activity that they ultimately understood to be for their benefit.

Crib sheets

Another way to provide WCF is through the use of marking or 'crib sheets'. A teacher could read through pupils' classwork and instead of writing comments in each individual book, they can make a set of notes, collating the feedback to give to the class during the next lesson.

The notes can include the following:

- **Areas of strength among the class.** This can include areas of strength demonstrated by specific individuals that can be recorded and shown to the rest of the class as examples to illustrate what excellence looks like. This could be 'what went well' (WWW).

- **Subject specific areas for improvement.** These may include common mistakes, misconceptions or any confusion that needs to be dealt with.
- **Feedback focusing on literacy.** This can range from spelling, punctuation and grammar to the use of key vocabulary.
- **Targets to help students move forward.** This can be noted as 'Even Better If' (EBI).
- **A record of any pupils of concern with incomplete work or demonstrating a lack of effort**. Individual conversations can then take place. It is important that pupils understand WCF is not a way for them to avoid individual accountability.

The crib sheet can include these points but may vary depending on the class, topic or subject; the feedback will then be shared with the class. The method of delivery can also vary, from the teacher providing verbal feedback based on their notes or crib sheet to presenting their comments to the class. Teachers will have to use their professional judgement when deciding how to share their notes, but WCF should never be used in a way that could potentially embarrass or humiliate pupils.

Greg Thornton, assistant headteacher and teacher of history, created a crib sheet as a way to support his own workload and provide more efficient feedback in his classes. Thornton shared this on social media and via his blog (mrthorntonteach.com) and this has since inspired and supported many other class teachers.

The following is a version of a crib sheet created and shared by Thornton.

History marking crib sheet **Date:** **Class:**

Praise:	Missing/incomplete work:	SPaG errors:
Cause for concern:	Misconceptions: Actions:	Presentation:
Polaroid moments:		

Thornton's crib sheet includes areas to record misconceptions, SPaG errors, missing work and praise. The 'polaroid moments' are successful snapshots that highlight excellence. The grid is a fantastic example of how WCF can be communicated to the class while holding learners to account and offering support and actionable feedback to move learning forwards.

Feedback grids

Using Greg Thornton's crib sheet as inspiration, generic feedback grids, such as the following example, can be used to deliver WCF or can be used for peer or self-assessment by learners.

What went well…	**Even better if…**
Questions…	**Next steps…**

In the example grid, the top two boxes focus on areas of strength and areas for development. The teacher can complete these based on reviewing class books and making a note of general trends. The questions box can support the teacher with lesson planning, helping them to prepare questions to revisit or ask the class. If the grids are being used by pupils for self-assessment they can make a record of any questions they would like answered; if the grid is being completed as part of peer assessment the pupil can write down questions for their peer to answer based on their work. The final box, 'next steps', can include targets or an actionable task.

The categories in the grid can be adapted to link with success criteria or include subject specific prompts. The main concept of the grid, similar to the example created by Thornton, is to provide a template for the teacher to record reflections and feedback when reviewing classwork and to assist with the communication of WCF to pupils.

There are challenges with marking and feedback for all teachers, but the challenges can vary between primary and secondary schools. Initially, WCF was promoted as a secondary school approach, but many primary schools have now embraced the method. The following case study focuses on Stanley Road Primary School in Oldham, Manchester, where WCF has been used for many years. WCF has become embedded as part of their school teaching, learning and assessment culture.

I have had the privilege to visit Stanley Road Primary School, and I was so impressed with the excellent behaviour, enthusiasm and attitudes towards learning and the slick routines that were firmly in place. I was able to observe lessons – from EYFS to Year 6 – that included feedback delivered verbally to individuals in the moment and in the lesson, as well as WCF delivered through the use of mini whiteboards to check for understanding.

Case study: WCF in a primary school

Bio: Andrew Percival is deputy head leading on curriculum and English at Stanley Road Primary School in Oldham. You can follow Andrew on X @primarypercival and he blogs at http://primarypercival.weebly.com/

The Forth Bridge is an iconic structure that spans a distance of 2.5km across the Firth of Forth in Scotland. The bridge is famous for the colloquial phrase 'painting the Forth Bridge' – this saying comes from the erroneous belief that the bridge was so huge it would need to be continually painted to maintain its upkeep. Such a practice never existed. In 2011, a new coating designed to last 25 years was applied to the Forth Bridge. The engineer Colin Hardie of Balfour Beatty Construction was quoted as saying, 'For the first time in the bridge's history there will be no painters required on the bridge. Job done.'

I never really questioned the value of marking. It was something you just did. Of course, children need their books marked. What else are we supposed to do with their books? Spending holidays catching up with marking that I had neglected was annoying but self-inflicted. I resented it but I knew it was my own fault for not using my time more effectively. When it came to light during an Ofsted inspection that a colleague hadn't marked their books for six months, we were all stunned. How on earth could you not mark your books? It was heresy!

Like painting the Forth Bridge, written marking is a seemingly never-ending task. As you complete that pile of books on a Sunday evening you know full well that Monday will bring a fresh new pile of books waiting to be analysed and responded to (possibly using a particular colour of ink and a range of highlighters). Marking is iconic. For many it is an impressive superstructure towering over teachers' day-to-day lives. It stands firm and unmoving despite changes in the educational weather.

The phrase 'painting the Forth Bridge' passed into everyday use despite never being founded on evidence. Can we now begin to say the same for the convention of written marking? I became increasingly aware of schools across the country eschewing traditional marking policies in favour of 'no written marking' approaches. Through exploring and reflecting on a range of teaching and learning blogs I began to doubt the impact of what I had spent many hundreds of hours of my teaching career doing, namely marking books with written comments.

When the EEF Teaching and Learning Toolkit was published, as a school we fell into the trap that many did of conflating marking with feedback. This led to an overemphasis on written marking at the expense of other forms of feedback. Written marking became king. We tinkered with the idea of dialogic marking, where teachers responded to a pupil's work, children responded to that response and so on. We were bolstered by the fact that our outcomes across the school were rapidly improving, so it seemed a reasonable assumption that our marking policy was part of this success.

As I read more widely, I became aware that the marking we asked teachers to undertake was perhaps not having the impact we had convinced ourselves it was having. The words of teacher and school leader Joe Kirby (2017) rang loudly in my ear: 'Written marking is useful for one child, once only.' What if all the hours spent marking each week could be used for something else? And what if we could actually improve the quality of feedback to pupils without the Sisyphean task of written marking?

The concerns with our system of marking were three-fold:

- Was the quality of feedback really as good as it could be? Were children really able to understand how the teacher wanted them to improve from a brief written comment? Were teachers compromising their feedback by truncating complex ideas into short comments with child-friendly language?

- Were children really taking responsibility for improving their own learning? Or were they relying on teachers to identify their errors and then simply responding to the teacher's marking? (For example, by filling in missing full stops that had been helpfully located by the conscientious teacher.)
- Were teachers so bogged down with the constant pressure to mark that they were unable to spend time on more valuable activities? Were teachers able to thoughtfully adapt their planning in light of feedback received or create high quality resources that could be used again and again? (We also had an inkling that staff who were completely burned out from an eternal marking pile might not actually make the very best teachers.)

At the end of the summer term we started to have serious conversations about replacing the current marking policy. We knew that Ofsted were not looking for a specific type of marking but were merely checking consistency of approach and that schools were able to achieve outstanding grades in an inspection despite being advocates of 'no written marking' policies. The 'Marking and other myths' document (2016) clarifies that:

> Ofsted does not expect to see any specific frequency, type or volume of marking and feedback; these are for the school to decide through its assessment policy. Marking and feedback should be consistent with that policy.

As we began the new academic year in September, we took the decision to design a new feedback policy that removed the need for written comments in books and implemented a more effective system of giving WCF at the start of the next lesson. We decided to trial this using the following broad approach.

After a lesson, the teacher looks through the pupils' books for common misconceptions and errors in basic skills. They then sort the books into three piles:

1. Children who didn't grasp the concept that was taught.
2. Children who showed good understanding.
3. Children who did particularly well.

Teachers tick each piece of work to show it has been checked and 'star' any parts of work that are worth sharing as good examples. While looking through the books, teachers make notes on the key messages to give feedback to pupils at the start of the next lesson using a grid, such as the following example.

Whole class feedback sheet **Lesson: English**

Work to praise and share	Need further support
Saba – excellent vocabulary choices Anees – description in opening (show under visualiser) Sophie – great dialogue (show under visualiser)	Hayden, Tanima, Aqib – noun/verb agreement weak, check through with adult during lesson Selena, Tom – not finished Josie – absent
Presentation	**Basic skills errors**
Great Show Sophie's book – good example of setting out speech and correct punctuation placement Reagan, Lena – errors not corrected with a single ruler line	Correct placement of punctuation at the end of direct speech is poor – model next lesson with Sophie's book Spellings • extraordinary • unconscious • symbol Teach and check with mini whiteboards

Misconceptions and next lesson notes
Problems with tense – swapping from past at start to present later on (e.g. Jack's work), need to re-teach key points from previous lesson. Next lesson – show these sentences and identify the error: 'The car skidded to a halt in front of the town hall. A tall man gets out and runs towards me.' Rewrite on whiteboards then check own work for errors with tense. Harley, Safa, Mariyah have no tense errors – complete challenge task identifying errors in levels of formality.

This book checking process should take no more than 15 minutes for a set of 30 books, and where possible children will have already marked their own work in the lesson to speed up this analysis (particularly in subjects like mathematics).

After this, the teacher plans a WCF session using the notes from the sheet as an aide-mémoire. The start of the next lesson begins with the teacher sharing the best work (perhaps using a visualiser), identifying common errors in basic skills (for example, spellings or number facts) and then addressing common misconceptions that have been identified. This session can be flexible in how long it takes, but a typical session might be 10 minutes or so, giving time for children to redress any misconceptions that have arisen and, where useful, check through their work and improve it based on the feedback given.

After running our trial for a few weeks, we decided to make a change to the nomenclature for our approach. Instead of 'whole class feedback sheets/sessions', we felt it better reflected what was actually happening in class to rename these as simply 'feedback sheets/sessions'. We ensure that verbal feedback before the next lesson meets the needs of individuals, groups and the whole class. For example, during the trial some teachers would give feedback to individuals on entry to the class, briefly talk to any groups and then provide the WCF.

We are now in the throes of the trial, and it would be naïve of me to speak authoritatively on the impact this is having on children's learning. One thing I can be fairly certain of, however, is the immediate and profound impact on teachers' workload. For a start, our teachers have happily reported to me that they no longer need to take books home to mark. Claire Hill (2017) strategic director at Steplab, states:

> Teachers are a school's most expensive resource, so our time is, quite literally, too valuable to waste on practices that are inefficient. But being efficient doesn't take any of the love or soul out of teaching; it gives us more time, energy and knowledge to deliver really great lessons.

> Let's be clear – we are in no way pioneers of this approach. Many schools have gone before us and have thankfully blogged about their approaches with great clarity and conviction. In a way, it is reassuring that a 'normal' primary school like ours is able to make such a move away from established practices to improve the quality of feedback and reduce teachers' workload. There is perhaps hope for other schools.
>
> Is a time coming when headteachers across the land might echo the words of Colin Hardie as he applied that final coat of durable epoxy paint to the Forth Bridge: 'For the first time in history, there will be no written marking required in books. Job done.'

There are lots of other examples of primary schools embracing WCF. Sophie Law is a Year 6 teacher at St Matthew's Catholic Primary in Bradford and an Evidence Lead in Education for Huntington Research School. Law (2021) reflects on her use of WCF:

> The time saved from written marking allowed for better preparation for the next lesson. Around 75% of children addressed errors in their books during that lesson, whereas before only 20% of children would respond to commentary. Children were able to ask questions about the improvements and develop discussions to deepen their understanding. On a single sheet of paper, I can see the bigger picture on how lessons went, and I had a record to reflect back on.

When introducing WCF in a primary context, it is a good idea to begin with English and maths. Teachers can trial and adapt WCF and follow up with careful reflection and review before applying it to other subjects.

Although feedback is central to every subject, it does vary across different subjects. Practical-based subjects will rely more heavily on verbal feedback; a PE teacher, for example, will constantly be providing pupils with feedback and guidance while observing their performance and progress. A teacher of languages will model and provide verbal feedback to support students to develop their speaking and listening skills. In terms of content to mark, there is a significant difference between subjects like maths in comparison with English and the humanities.

For subjects that require teachers to read lengthy essays and assessments, WCF can be a game changer. As an experienced teacher of history and politics I have spent a lot of time reading extensive essays and exam papers, and I have found this overwhelming and challenging at times. For many years I accepted this was part of my job and there simply was no other way. I was very wrong. I would have benefited immensely in the early years of my teaching career from using workload-friendly feedback strategies such as WCF.

Another history teacher who can relate to my struggles with feedback and marking is Derrick Roberts. In the following case study, Derrick reflects on the transition to WCF and the impact of this on his workload and his learners' outcomes.

Case study: WCF in history

Bio: Derrick Roberts is a teacher of history and principal teacher of teaching and learning at a secondary school in the Scottish Highlands. He is active on X @MrRobHistory.

Over my 20 plus years of teaching, marking and feedback has been a constant difficulty. I've had so many CPD sessions on how to mark books, covering various methods including the following:

- Two stars and a wish.
- Only positive feedback allowed.
- Marking in green because it is less confrontational.

However, nothing has ever seemed to make a dent in the two problems I have found with marking and feedback: first, the massive workload and pressure it places on teachers who often spend hours and hours working late into the night to get it done; and second, making sure that feedback is encouraging, effective and helpful for our students to move towards their goals and progress in their work. The problem I have found with written feedback is that students very rarely have the chance to read it, and given it is often a negative experience I wondered why they would want to read the feedback in the first place. It's bit like receiving a letter from HMRC; it could be good news, but we are still nervous to open it.

So, in the last couple of years, I have been trying to find a better way to mark books – a way which reduces workload but also provides quality and effective feedback. I am active on X and often find some very useful resources on there; one evening I came across a post written by Greg Thornton discussing whole class feedback, and was so impressed I decided to give his approach a try.

The process is very simple: I select a number of books – between a quarter and a third – from each class and mark them really well, making sure to follow the school's policy and look for positives and misconceptions. I then record the findings on a crib sheet. This crib sheet has sections where I record the common misconceptions, SPaG errors and examples of what they did well. I also record, for my own information, any students who are giving me cause for concern, and I make sure that I find time for individual conversations with these students.

I follow this up with some slides for the next lesson's presentation that highlights the common errors as well as things that went well. These are presented and discussed with all students during the lesson. They then carry out a DIRT activity and think about the things they did, as well as any common errors they may have made, and they reflect on how these points will help improve their learning going forward. I also record myself giving this feedback and upload the audio file to the Google Classroom, so any students who are absent can also hear the feedback.

The following benefits of this process have been remarkable for myself, my students and the curriculum.

- The workload has been reduced considerably. The whole process of marking, recording and creating slides for feedback takes me about 45 minutes rather than the couple of hours it used to take. The provision of the feedback and DIRT takes another 15 minutes in class. I have found myself able to mark the work of more classes.

- The quality of the feedback has improved dramatically. I am now able to highlight and correct common misconceptions and demonstrate the best ways to achieve learning objectives, and all students are now given time to reflect on the feedback rather than having to quickly glance at some written comments when they have a moment.
- Student work is improving as a result of this. The time allowed for reflection helps them to identify steps for success and errors that they might try to avoid. Having the DIRT sheet in their class books also helps as a visual reminder. I have seen certain misconceptions become rarer and rarer and the strengths identified become more and more common.
- The marking and feedback have also helped improve the quality of my curriculum as well. It has helped identify common misconceptions and literacy errors. I am able to take the crib sheets to department meetings and discuss the findings; these then help to make changes to teaching to emphasise what is going well and to change how we teach certain things to ensure that the misconceptions arise less and less.

The process isn't perfect, but it has helped me so much as a teacher. I am under less pressure, I am actually marking more and the students are getting better feedback that is driving improvement in their learning. I am convinced that this process of WCF is one of the biggest changes I have made to my teaching in the last two years, and something I will absolutely be continuing with.

The Mountain Ash Comprehensive School (MACS) Teaching and Learning blog reflects on the use of WCF, writing:

> The pedagogical impact of WCF extends beyond the obvious points for improvement for learners. [...] There can be consideration for changes to curriculum design and delivery and informing short- and medium-term planning. In essence marking becomes planning, which is fundamentally a better use of valuable time.

Reviewing classwork and preparing feedback with WCF for the next lesson also enables responsive teaching. This can help the teacher to plan their next lesson, whether students have understood a concept, and the learning can move forwards, or they have some confusion that must be addressed before progressing further. Ultimately, WCF is an approach that fully embodies formative assessment.

English teacher and writer Adam Riches (2019) observes criticisms of WCF:

> [Critics argue that] this approach destroys individualised feedback and can hinder the highest attainers' progress, due to them not having a misconception in the first place. Those concerns are valid, but only if WCF is used badly. [...] When done well, WCF can save hours of teacher time and actually significantly improve student outcomes. But it is in danger of being seen as a fad because it is being misunderstood.

Like all or most strategies and techniques in education, WCF can be vulnerable to 'lethal mutation'. This is a term coined by Ed Haertel (Brown and Campione, 1996), and it refers to an idea, concept or practice that is grounded in robust evidence but has then been implemented in a way that damages its effectiveness. Deep understanding and knowledge of the evidence or the strategy, in addition to regular reflection can help avoid the 'lethal mutations' occurring in the classroom.

It is important to reflect on this approach and the impact it has on student learning and progress. WCF should be used alongside other feedback strategies, and it should be considered in the context of the age group, key stage and subject domain.

Case Study: WCF in A level PE

Bio: Matthew Anglesea is assistant principal and an experienced teacher of A level PE at Durham Sixth Form Centre.

I am currently the sole teacher of A level PE, teaching the whole specification areas across years 12 and 13. My average class size is 24. The school's teaching, learning and assessment policy outlines that where knowledge is assessed by an external examination, we aim to provide quality feedback on a minimum of two pieces of substantial written work per subject every half term.

The policy suggests staff should give students time to ask questions about the marked work, as well as time to respond to feedback in a meaningful way and signpost future actions. This should enable students to articulate what they need to do to improve. There is no expectation that these responses are then remarked; instead, we would expect staff to respond to gaps in knowledge and address these as part of 'quality first' teaching. The policy is influenced by the argument put forward by Wiliam and Leahy (2015): 'Feedback, no matter how well designed, that the student does not act upon is a waste of time.'

I have used a WCF approach for the last five to six years. I was initially influenced by Adam Boxer's blog on evidence-based practice in marking and feedback (2018), along with the time I was spending writing the same comment on every piece of work I marked. The substantive written work in my subject often involves an 8- or 15-mark essay question. The essays are marked against three assessment outcomes: AO1 – Knowledge; AO2 – Application; and AO3 – Analysis/Evaluation. I give their work a level, as opposed to a raw mark.

As I work through marking I make general notes on the strengths and common errors that students are making. Once finished, I then use my notes to produce a WCF sheet using the following steps.

- I identify what the focus of AO1, AO2 and AO3 was.
- I then identify 'highlights' (these are the common strengths) and 'common errors' (this includes what students did or didn't do that cost them marks). I include a section titled 'top sentences'.
- I provide the students with at least three examples of what they have written that enabled them to access AO1, AO2 and AO3 marks.
- I use the examples to reinforce the points identified in the highlights and common errors section.
- I then identify next steps (normally three); these will be differentiated, and I will highlight which steps I want students to do.

These next steps will focus on correcting and consolidating knowledge, redrafting a section to access AO3 or a challenge to apply their understanding to something novel or synoptic. I provide lesson time for students to do this, and during that time students can ask questions and clarify misconceptions. In an ideal world I would be able to read and feed back on their improvements. However, due to curriculum and time constraints this is not possible. I have to be targeted and varied with the students I focus on during this time.

What I have recently started to do is consolidate this part of the lesson with a hinge question. I give consideration to any potential misconceptions that may have been evident in the students' written work and then design a hinge question that has the potential to reassure me that the misconceptions have been addressed and as a group we are ready to move on.

I recommend reading the blogs on hinge questioning by Harry Fletcher-Wood; they have been really helpful when trying to design a purposeful hinge question. I use Plickers, an online formative assessment tool, as a platform to ask the hinge question. Plickers immediately provides the percentage of correct answers, alongside who got it right and wrong, so I can make the decision to move on or consolidate further within seconds. It also records the data so I can go back and use it to inform future lessons.

Students speak positively about my approach to feedback lessons, as they appreciate the examples of good practice and the opportunities to improve their work and understanding. Below is an example of the whole class feedback provided to my pupils.

Using the data, evaluate the sociological and factors affecting female participation in football, athletics and tennis. (8 marks)		
✓ **A01 Knowledge** – Identification of sociological factor (stereotypes, socialisation, discrimination, social stratification). ✓✓ **A02 Application** – Linking the sociological factor to causing a barrier & use of data. ✓✓✓ **A03 Analysis/ Evaluation** – Identifying positives and negatives of female participation from the data and using sociological factors to explain why the data shows this.	**Highlights** Correct identification of the positives and negatives of female participation from the data. Starting paragraphs with what the data shows. Making synoptic links to historical developments: – Causes of female stereotypes. – Equality of pay in tennis. Linking low participation in tennis to social stratification and class.	**Common errors** Careless mistakes, talking about what the data shows but forgetting to name the sport you are talking about. The explanation as to what the data shows was superficial and lacked depth. Not enough connectives used to develop depth to the response.

Next steps	Top sentences
Reshape a paragraph on tennis, exploring why it has the fewest participation numbers but is the most equitable with males. Make reference to social stratification and stereotypes in your answer. Can you write a paragraph to explain using sociological factors, why swimming and fitness are two sports where females participate more than males?	*In the table there is a significant gap between the female and male participation in football. (1, 750,000 males and only 100,00 females.)* ***This could be due to a*** *lack of access for females, there are less female football clubs and competitions and facilities that welcome female footballers.* ***This leads to*** *the lack of participation of female players with the ability and potential so the standard of female football does not increase,* ***therefore*** *not increasing interest in spectators,* ***leading to*** *a lack of funding to be able to increase female opportunities. The lack of interest* ***means that*** *females do not get involved and teams cannot be formed as they need at least 11 female participants to increase club numbers and opportunities* ***therefore*** *participation numbers are low.* *In tennis, there is the smallest difference between the number of male and female participants which is* ***showing that*** *possibly tennis is more inclusive and has the least discrimination. Throughout the development of tennis, female participation has always been socially acceptable due to the emancipation of women and challenging such stereotypes.* ***This has caused*** *more women to progress in tennis and has* ***led to*** *more media coverage than football.* ***Resulting in*** *more role models for females to aspire to be like, encouraging them to participate in tennis.* ***However,*** *there are still more males that participate per week than females.* ***This could be due to*** *a lack of access to clubs and facilities which may* ***lead to*** *a decrease in motivation to participate as they may not have a high level of social stratification to afford travel expenses or child care* ***hence*** *decreasing female participation in tennis.* ***However****, from the data we can also see athletics has the highest number of female participants across the three sports.* ***This could be*** *because it's easier to participate as they don't have to wait for a full team* ***so it is*** *more accessible. Athletics also has more part in female PE provision,* ***resulting in*** *more females taking part in athletics in school and* ***therefore****, they keep participating even when they leave school.*

WCF is an efficient method of reviewing pupils' classwork and communicating feedback to learners. It can be very insightful for the teacher, identifying common misconceptions and gaps in knowledge, as well as highlighting general areas of strength. This can guide future lesson planning and enable responsive and adaptive teaching. WCF can also hold pupils to account, and individuals can still be identified by the teacher if they need further help or support.

WCF has been used for several years across schools; therefore, teachers and leaders are in a position where they can reflect on the impact this approach has had on pupil progress and teacher workload. The case studies in this chapter demonstrate how WCF can be implemented across different key stages, from primary up to A level, and across different subjects, from the humanities to PE.

Chapter summary

- When communicated clearly to the class with feedback that is understandable, helpful and actionable, WCF can support pupil progress and help to move learning forward.
- WCF can lead to meaningful and reflective conversations that focus on key areas of strength and areas for development.
- It is important that pupils engage with WCF and do not assume the feedback is not relevant or important to them. This can be addressed and explained by the teacher, and actionable tasks can be provided for learners.
- WCF has been shown to significantly reduce teacher workload. This is especially evident for essay-based subjects.
- There are different ways that technology can provide whole class feedback. This can vary from writing comments on a platform or virtual learning environment (VLE) that all learners have access, to using a classroom visualiser.

Chapter 4
Self-assessment

Reflection is not easy to do and not something pupils tend to do naturally, although it can and should become a study habit. Teachers need to guide, instruct, model and monitor self-assessment very carefully. There is a harmful misconception that self-assessment is a lazy approach to feedback.

In a previous book I authored, *Wiliam & Leahy's Five Formative Assessment Strategies in Action* (2021), I argued that encouraging pupils to be masters of their own learning was the holy grail of teaching and learning. I stand by this statement; self-assessment is an important element of an individual taking responsibility for their learning and progress.

All teaching and learning strategies should contribute and lead to the point where learners take ownership of their learning by monitoring their own progress and acting on feedback provided. This comes back to the idea covered in the introduction, that while teachers can spend copious amounts of time considering the feedback they provide, if the pupil ignores that feedback then it simply can't have any impact.

Self-assessment is another method of feedback and reflection that can enable learners to improve and make progress. As D. Royce Sadler (1989) argues:

> A key premise is that for students to be able to improve, they must develop the capacity to monitor the quality of their own work during actual production. [...] This in turn requires that students possess an appreciation of what high quality work is, that they have the evaluative skill necessary for them to compare

> with some objectivity the quality of what they are producing in relation to the higher standard, and that they develop a store of tactics or moves which can be drawn upon to modify their own work.

Self-assessment can be complex and challenging. Self-assessment and peer assessment (which will be discussed in chapter 5) need to be closely monitored, guided and supported by the teacher. The teacher plays a very important role in pupil assessment, although teachers should hope to become redundant so learners can eventually become confident in self-assessment without the need for explicit guidance and supervision.

Research has shown (Chin, 2016) that learners can be prone to over- or underestimating their abilities and achievements when taking part in self-assessment, relative to their assessment of others. This is an important point for teachers to be aware of when providing opportunities for self-assessment, and is one of the reasons why teacher guidance and monitoring is essential.

The EEF published the 'Metacognition and Self-regulated Learning Guidance Report' in 2018 (updated in 2021). The report explains that 'self-regulated learners are aware of their strengths and weaknesses, and can motivate themselves to engage in, and improve, their learning.'

Clearly, feedback plays an important and central role in being a self-regulated learner. And yet a problem with self-assessment and being a self-regulated learner is the challenge to be able to accurately identify areas of strength and weakness. The EEF highlights this point:

> One issue that pupils often have with independent learning is their accuracy of judgement. They tend not to have very realistic views of how well they have learned something, or which strategy has been effective. Consequently, they can make unrealistic 'judgements of learning'.

When I began teaching, a widely used method of self-assessment (or Assessment for Learning (AfL)) teachers were encouraged to use was 'RAG rating'. This involved asking learners to use the traffic light colours red, amber and green to self-assess. Red usually represented difficulty, amber meant unsure and green meant great. RAG ratings are still used in schools, but they are not as fashionable as they once were.

Why have we moved away from the traffic light system in the classroom? Possibly because learners can struggle to accurately self-assess their level of knowledge or understanding. For example, a pupil might pick a green pen to tick their work because they feel confident and happy they have understood the lesson content, although they may have unknowingly misunderstood a key concept or made several mistakes. Another pupil might select red as their chosen colour, but it may be the case that although all of their answers are correct, they struggle with self-esteem and often doubt their abilities.

The traffic light system has its flaws, but with clear guidance and access to success and assessment criteria there can still be a place in the classroom for RAG, as shown in some of the examples in this chapter.

Where? How? Next steps?

Hattie and Timperley (2007) have advised teachers to ask their pupils to consider three key questions when they receive feedback. The questions, which the pupils answer, with support from the teacher, are shown in the template below.

Where am I going?	How am I going?	What is the next step?

Hattie has written about the importance of these questions, with the first question focusing on where the learning is going. Hattie (2011) writes, 'When students understand their goals and what success at those goals look like, then the feedback is more powerful.'

The second question is one that pupils can refer to throughout the learning process. Hattie explains that this is related to progress feedback and how it can be reflective about past or present performance. The final question is linked to targets and actionable feedback, addressing what the pupil should do next in order to progress.

These questions can be rephrased to suit the learners in the classroom; for example, the first question could be phrased as: 'What is the goal?' The pupils can be aware of these questions, or they can have the template in their books to fill in at different stages of the learning process.

The first box will link with the learning intentions. Educational scientist and author Pedro De Bruyckere (2018) has highlighted the importance of setting and explaining clear goals, objectives and intentions for learners. De Bruyckere asks:

> How can you give feedback if you can't see whether or not someone has reached the set objective? […] The objectives must be the yardstick you use to measure the pupils' performance and the feedback you give will deal with the extent to which they have achieved these objectives (or not) and how they can do better next time.

Teachers should ensure the objectives and learning intentions are challenging and desirably difficult, while also making sure they are achievable. The questions suggested by Hattie and Timperley encourage pupils to take responsibility for and ownership of their learning at three important stages: planning, monitoring and evaluating. This demonstrates that self-assessment is an ongoing process, not something to be carried out at the last minute before submitting classwork to the teacher.

Four quarters marking

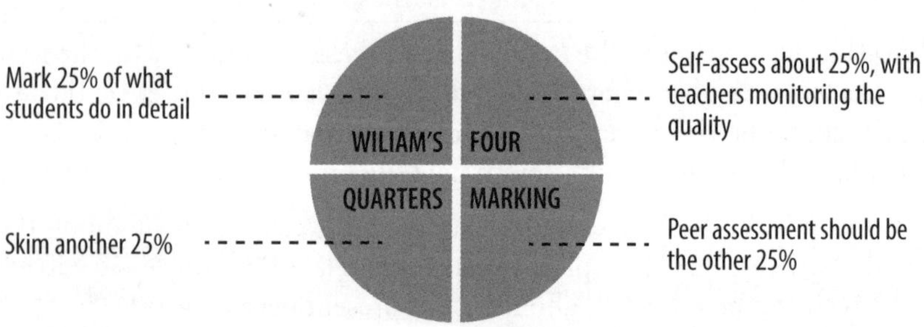

The 'four quarters marking' model developed by Dylan Wiliam (2017) is a straightforward concept that can be applied across different subjects and key stages. The model provides school leaders, teachers, pupils and parents with guidance about feedback provided in the classroom that can support learners, while also offering a solution to the workload burden caused by excessive marking.

According to Wiliam, classroom teachers should mark 25% of classwork in detail (this can include written comments, marking codes or WCF). Another 25% of pupils' work can be skimmed. General classwork will be scanned to inform the teacher while they are checking for understanding and accountability of the pupils, while also identifying areas for development. Verbal feedback can also be given to pupils as the teacher circulates around the classroom.

When classwork is scanned by the teacher, a standard 'tick and flick' method has been common practice in class books for decades. The tick and flick concept is simple: the tick represents that the teacher has flicked through the class book and reviewed the pupil's work. This serves a purpose: to tell the learner their work has been read and checked. A tick can provide feedback, which is usually a confirmation that pupils have answered questions correctly or completed their work accurately. The tick and flick approach is obviously very limited in terms of the feedback it can offer pupils to move their learning forwards.

The second half of Wiliam's model focuses on pupil feedback. Learners should self-assess about 25% of classwork with the teacher supporting and monitoring the quality of their assessment. The final 25% should be represented by peer assessment, again with accompanying instruction and support. As mentioned previously, peer and self-assessment are not always easy to implement and embed as these methods often pose many challenges for the pupils attempting to enact them effectively.

The percentages offered by Wiliam are indicative and not to be fixated on. It is important that teachers within a department agree which classwork will be marked in detail and which pieces should be scanned or peer or self-assessed by pupils. This will ensure consistency and transparency across classes and departments. Wiliam describes this as 'a sort of balanced diet of different kinds of marking and assessment.'

The four quarters marking model offers useful advice without being prescriptive with a specific time period (for example, 'work must be marked every two weeks'). The teacher can implement the model in the required context and use their professional judgement to decide which type of feedback should be provided and when.

Michael Chiles echoes this sentiment about variety. Chiles (2020) writes:

> For feedback to be effective, it should be [carried out] through a variety of different forms that [form] part of an ongoing process. It should be something that is not allocated a timescale. For this to happen, teachers should have the autonomy to provide feedback as and when it is needed. For this to happen teachers should be equipped with the strategies that will enable them to recognise when pupils need feedback.

In terms of introducing this policy in a school, Wiliam (2017) advises,

> I would say first of all, headteachers should lay down clear expectations to parents and say things like, 'We are not going to give detailed feedback on more than 25% of what your child does. The reason for that is not because we're lazy. It's because there are better uses we could make of that time. We could mark everything your child does, but that would lead to lower quality teaching and then your child will learn less.' Heads have to establish those cultural norms. If a teacher is marking everything your child does, it's bad teaching. It is using time in a way that does not have the greatest benefit for students.

As head of department, I was able to introduce Wiliam's policy at a departmental level. I explained the concept with my colleagues, and we agreed it would be the approach we would adopt to provide feedback. We would regularly discuss upcoming work and how that would be assessed in departmental meetings.

Departmental meetings can often be dominated by administrative tasks, but I always ensured 'reflection' was added to the meeting agenda, despite time restrictions. The focus of this reflection would vary from behaviour to assessment and, of course, feedback. It is important to reflect as individual classroom teachers, at a departmental and whole-school level.

The following are examples of reflection questions to consider:

- **Are there any challenges with feedback? If so, what are they and how can we resolve them?**
- **What feedback strategies, techniques or approaches are working well? How do we know this?**

- **How are pupils responding to feedback, and are they acting on feedback provided?**

Dr Carl Hendrick (2017) has written about the four quarters marking model as being a workload solution. Hendrick states:

> As a profession, we are to some extent our own worst enemy. Using marking policies that have little impact on student achievement and a negative impact on teacher workload and morale makes little sense. By adopting an approach like four quarters marking, we might go some way to address this issue and at the same time give students more ownership over their own learning.

I have shared the four quarters marking approach with schools I have worked with around the world. One school I was fortunate to visit and lead INSET training at was El Limonar International School (ELIS) in Murcia, Spain. The following case study by classroom teacher Alysha Ali describes how the four quarters marking approach has been applied at ELIS.

Case study: Four quarter marking in action

Bio: Alysha Ali is a teacher of history and head of faculty (humanities) at ELIS in Murcia, Spain.

History in our school has become one of the highest performing subjects at A level and IGCSE. When questioned about results, it is surprising to people when I state that teacher marking is only found on extended writing or exam-style questions. This is a result of our whole-school policy following Dylan Wiliam's four quarter marking.

In our department, the approach ensures that marking and feedback is not a post mortem of pupil work but rather offers a remedy, helping pupils feed-forward by providing challenge and promoting pupil agency as well as encouraging teachers to work smarter, saving valuable time.

The 25% of pupil work that should be self-assessed is achieved by pupils self-marking answers to retrieval starters that test prior knowledge. Answers are gauged through targeted questioning and are displayed clearly on the board with time given for pupils to self-mark and correct. Over time, this has become routine for pupils who are provided with instantly modelled verbal and visual feedback.

Self-assessment is also used to ensure pupils are submitting quality extended writing for teacher marking. When marking traditionally, teachers often duplicate comments. To reduce this, at the end of allocated essay writing time pupils are provided with crib sheets with an excellent high-level paragraph example alongside mini success criteria. By benchmarking their work against high-level examples, pupils are empowered with the tools and skills to revisit their work, identifying where they have hit the criteria along with points for improvement, ticking or crossing the sheet as they go. Pupils then spend time filling in or correcting missing elements, which allows them to instantly upskill and reflect on their work. Though this process can take extended lesson time, it is time saving as less traditional marking is required, because pupils are submitting quality work that is the best they can produce.

The 25% involving teacher marking is dedicated to exam-style answers or extended writing. Our focus is predominantly on ensuring teacher feedback invites a pupil response, helping them to close the gap between their current level of work and excellent work. We write comments on the body of the work, providing hints or next steps. The main principle is that any teacher marking must invite responses.

To avoid overloading the work – and therefore the pupil – with too many comments or written feedback, we make use of pre-made simplified mark schemes that can be used repeatedly, thus lessening workload. Teachers simply highlight criteria that have been achieved and at least one actionable 'even better if' point, out of multiple pre-composed points. This significantly reduces the number of prompts a teacher writes on the work. To close the feedback loop, pupils are handed back their marked work and given time for reflection and redrafting, where they respond to teacher prompts by improving a section of their work in a designated space on the page, ensuring feedback is actively used.

The penultimate 25% is made up of light-touch marking. Here, we use sample marking. Teachers periodically take a mixed-attainment sample of pupil books, browsing for common misconceptions and areas for development. These points are turned into open questions on a review sheet that's provided to pupils. It is explained to pupils how these questions are derived and what their purpose is. Pupils are given a lesson to go through their books and be detectives, attempting to identify which questions they can answer and what lessons the questions pertain to. Pupils then find space on the relevant lesson page, answering the questions and marking the answer with a reflection box.

Exemplar pupil answers are modelled, including via a visualiser. Expectations are highlighted through providing high-level benchmarks. Pupils therefore assess their learning in an active manner while simultaneously challenging themselves. It is also a powerful use of time, allowing for recapping and retesting of previously covered knowledge, as well as being a time saving technique.

Peer assessment makes up the final quarter. I have found this works best when examples are modelled prior to the task. Any of the retrieval self-assessment tasks can become peer assessment tasks with modelling. One method we use is a twist on the 'find and fix' retrieval activity. Pupils' brain dump 5–10 knowledge statements, leaving space between each one. They swap statements with a partner, who ticks any correct statements while finding and fixing any errors. Pupils are encouraged to enhance their partner's statement by adding more explanation, using 'what, who, when, where, why' as prompts.

As an alternative task, the marker can write prompts to invite a response from their partner. The prompts can be returned straight away and amended by the pupil, therefore closing the feedback-loop, or left until a later date and revisited as a starter activity. This allows for clear peer assessment while being workload friendly and a powerful retrieval tool.

> The four quarters marking policy has been instrumental in supporting teacher workload; it means that we rarely physically mark every student book. The quality feedback that is gleaned from this approach is purposeful, empowering pupil agency in their own learning as well as being a powerful source of retrieval and challenge that encourages pupil progress.

Dot marking

Dot marking is a simple idea and can easily be carried out in a lesson. This is a teacher-led technique, but the focus is on the learner to check their work and make adjustments and improvements as a form of reflection and self-assessment. Accordingly, I would categorise this approach as supported self-assessment.

In this method, the teacher simply places a dot in the margin (or near) where there is an error or an area of work in which the pupil can improve. A bingo dabber, dot stickers or any colour pen can be used. Some teachers and schools find it helpful to use the same colour pen to help students recognise the 'dot', but this isn't essential.

Different colour dots could represent different errors; for example, a green dot could signpost a literacy mistake and a blue dot could represent a factual inaccuracy. However, we have to be careful not to overcomplicate a simple technique as we always want the learners to understand the feedback and what they should do next.

The dot doesn't provide the learner with information about the mistake they have made; it simply highlights where the error is. This is similar to the detective strategy discussed previously. The dot has identified the error, and the onus is now on the pupil to rectify that error. This is a simple example of actionable feedback.

David Fawcett (2019) is an advocate of dot marking, writing:

> When teachers spot an error, there is the reflex to rectify it. Then we mark their books a few weeks later and see the same error again. But if we've done the correction for them, what have they actually learned? An easy way to overcome this is dot marking.

The teacher could put a dot on pupil work during a lesson while circulating around the classroom, or they could do so when reviewing class books after a lesson. Either way, the teacher must ensure the learner is aware of the dot and does something about it.

Amjad Ali has suggested a variation of dot marking with peer assessment. Ali (2014) suggests: 'Get students peer assessing using the dot marking method too. RAG rating dot marking – red, amber and green dots.'

Dot marking is very workload friendly as it is not time consuming. It is an example of feedback being more work for the learner than the teacher because as the dot tells the pupil to check their work, they are then compelled to reflect and correct. It is important to monitor this approach and provide further clarification with a written comment or a conversation if necessary to check the learner understands why the dot is on their classwork and what they should do next.

Dot targets

Another variation of dot marking focuses on 'dot targets'. This is where the teacher establishes a set of targets, and each pupil has the target assigned that is relevant to them. The colour dot on their classwork (as shown in the following example) indicates what they need to do next so they can act on the targets provided by the teacher.

- **Blue: Revisit your paragraph, focusing on literacy.** Check the accuracy of spellings and ensure capital letters and full stops are used correctly throughout.
- **Green: Revisit your paragraph, checking for factual accuracy.** Make sure you have used the correct terms in the correct context and that all facts, data and statistics are correct.
- **Yellow: Revisit your paragraph, adding more detail to support your points.** Consider how you can extend your points by adding further information that is relevant and accurate. What examples can you include?

The dot target task may not always be appropriate; for example, what about the pupils who have not presented any literacy or factual errors and have included relevant detail? They can be given a target, but it should genuinely challenge them, not simply be something extra for that learner to do.

Quizzing and self-assessment

Quizzing serves a range of purposes and can be used at different stages of the learning process. Quizzing is one method of eliciting evidence of learning, and it can be used across key stages and subjects to check for understanding, help consolidate new knowledge and identify any misconceptions. Quizzing can also be used at a later date with learners as an opportunity to recall answers and information from long-term memory, allowing retrieval practice to take place.

An important distinction teachers should be aware of is that of learning versus performance (Bjork and Bjork, 1992). Performance demonstrates whether to-be-learned knowledge or skills can be produced during the instruction phase itself, but this is not always a reliable indicator of learning. The Bjorks argue that what teachers can measure during the instruction process in a lesson is performance, but not (yet) learning.

Quizzes carried out during the initial stages of the learning process, for example at the end of a lesson with questions based on the content covered, help to assess pupil performance. Performance can be dependent on cues that are present during the lesson but are unlikely to be present at a later time in a different context, when some skill or knowledge is required.

Bjork and Bjork (2011) write that:

> We can be misled by our current performance. Conditions of learning that make performance improve rapidly often fail to support long-term retention and transfer, whereas conditions that create challenges and slow the rate of apparent learning often optimise long-term retention and transfer.

To simplify, we can consider performance to check for understanding and use retrieval practice to check for long-term learning. This theory links with the well-known observation by Paul A. Kirschner, John Sweller and Richard E. Clark (2006), who note that learning occurs when there is a change in long-term memory.

A quiz shouldn't be created to be used once with a class. Instead, schools should have a collection of question banks that can be given to pupils in a variety of ways. Quizzes should be repeated not for workload purposes (although this can support teacher workload), but mainly because they provide the class with regular opportunities to answer questions and make progress.

Teachers can assess and mark quizzes, but this is not the best approach to help learners in terms of engaging with feedback and is also not the best option in terms of teacher workload. Wiliam (2017) has advised that the best person to mark a test is the person who has just taken it. This is great advice for teachers and pupils, and was transformative in my own teaching practice as I realised how important and useful it was for my learners to be involved in the feedback process, especially with quizzing.

The teacher can provide WCF and present the answers to the class – this is time efficient and effective. The pupils also have an opportunity to engage with the feedback and reflect on their progress. Through self-assessment, pupils can identify areas of strength and gaps in their knowledge.

Retrieval practice tasks lend themselves very well to peer and self-assessment, as well as another element of marking not included in the four quarters model – online marking. This encompasses tools or websites that mark and score quizzes and instantly provide the teacher and pupils with results and feedback.

I have written extensively about retrieval practice, and I encourage teachers to take a 'low effort, high impact' approach to implementing and embedding retrieval practice. The low effort is for the teacher; retrieval practice must be low effort in terms of planning and feedback because retrieval practice should become established as a regular classroom routine, and so it must be workload friendly and sustainable for teachers.

The emphasis is low effort, not no effort, as there will be effort from teachers for careful planning, question design and monitoring. The high impact element focuses on pupil learning to ensure long-term memory is strengthened through regular retrieval, which allows learners to access information quickly, confidently and correctly.

An issue that can occur with quizzing in the classroom is the tendency for learners to focus on their scores. A pupil may be happy with a quiz score of 25 out of 30, but knowing the score alone is not enough. The pupil needs to find out and understand the five errors they made so they do not repeat those mistakes in the future. Through self-assessment, the pupil will be able to clearly see the correct and incorrect answers in front of them.

Mini whiteboards are ideal for quizzing with multiple choice and short answer questions. The teacher can view a class set of responses and provide immediate WCF. If my pupils were unsure of an answer or didn't know what to write, I advised them to draw a large question mark on their mini whiteboard. When the boards were shown I could see if there were question marks, and I could then deal with these questions and support the learners who were unsure of something.

Quizzes can be peer assessed (this will be discussed in more detail in the next chapter), although in terms of retrieval practice quizzing I promote the use of self-assessment over peer assessment. The main reason for this is that retrieval practice should be a low stakes task designed to increase retrieval strength, making information easier and quicker (and therefore more recallable) in the future. Self-assessment supports the low stakes nature of retrieval practice, while peer assessment can possibly increase the stakes as learners may be worried about their peer knowing their score.

However, this is just my advice, and once again the effectiveness of feedback depends on many variables, including the culture of the classroom and the individuals within the class. The best person to make an informed decision about the best feedback method to use is ultimately the teacher.

Carousel Learning

Carousel is an innovative online quizzing tool designed to help teachers teach smarter and support pupils to learn better. Quizzing with Carousel aims to embed pupil knowledge in long-term memory and reduce teacher workload.

Carousel continues to grow in popularity, as more teachers and schools are subscribing to the various packages on offer (ranging from a free plan to upgraded paid subscriptions). Carousel is available for both primary and secondary schools and has curricular materials for all subjects. A plan can be used by individual teachers, departments or across a whole school or MAT.

Carousel has also developed in terms of the features it offers. Teachers can upload or create their own question banks as well as gain access to editable community banks that have been professionally produced and are quality assured. Carousel is very versatile as it can be used in a lesson combined with mini whiteboards (if your school has limited access to technology, this is ideal). The teacher can skim and scan a class set of answers, which can become part of a consistent classroom routine to provide opportunities for retrieval practice.

Online quizzes can also be set if pupils have access to devices in the classroom. Carousel is designed to support retrieval practice outside of the classroom through homework and revision. Quizzes can be set by the teacher and pupils can study using the flashcards (the questions are converted into flashcard format) before taking a quiz. Pupils can attempt a quiz more than once, providing plentiful opportunities for consolidation and later retrieval practice. The teacher can also find out if pupils have completed the quiz or not.

In terms of feedback, there are a variety of ways Carousel can support pupils and teachers. Carousel offers learners the opportunity to self-assess and reflect on their answers. This is much more effective and meaningful than simply providing pupils with a total score that doesn't focus on or address gaps in knowledge. Pupils are shown the correct answer from the quiz, and they then compare it with their response, deciding if it was correct or incorrect.

Although self-assessment is promoted there is still accountability in place. If the pupil's answer is incorrect (and they will know this when the correct answer is shown to them) but they mark it as correct, this can be addressed as the teacher can oversee and monitor how pupils self-assess their answers. The teacher can change the answer from correct to incorrect.

If the teacher notices a common misconception, spelling error or answer that they feel they need to address with the class in the lesson, they can check the box to 'include in feedback' and it will be flagged up for later reference. Through selecting key questions to discuss with the class, Carousel lends itself well to WCF. The data provided to teachers after pupils have completed the quiz can highlight the questions the class found the most difficult, highlight the lowest score and indicate what percentage of the class achieved the average score. This again can be discussed and revisited with WCF.

The feedback provided from Carousel quizzes can help support responsive and adaptive teaching, informing future lesson planning. Adam Boxer is an experienced science teacher, author and director of education at Carousel. Boxer explains how Carousel's revolutionary C-Scores feature works:

> In the absence of strong teacher input, students might 'complete' homework in a technical sense – tick; done! – but they don't learn from it. Teachers need to be deeply embedded in the process of student knowledge growth: guiding, directing and, crucially, responding to student knowledge as it develops. C-Scores allow the computer to do what it does best – crunch numbers – and empower the teacher to do what they do best – figure out informed next steps for their students. Imagine knowing to a granular level exactly which things your students know well and which they don't. Imagine knowing when the last time they did retrieval on a particular item was, or when the last time they saw that item was. Imagine how it would affect and change your ability to plan next steps. C-Scores do all this and more. [...] C-Scores were a deliberate attempt to make Carousel even more adaptive and responsive to student learning, but they only mark the start of a wider strategy called Responsive Quizzing.

To find out more about Carousel Learn, visit https://www.carousel-learning.com/

'Do now' tasks

Doug Lemov (2014) has described a 'do now' task as the following:

> The first step in a great lesson is a do now – a short activity that you have written on the board or that is waiting for students as they enter. It often starts working before you do. While you are greeting students at the door, or finding that stack of copies, or erasing the mark-ups you made to your overhead from the last lesson, students should already be busy, via the do now, with scholarly work that prepares them to succeed. [...]

> In fact, students entering your room should never have to ask themselves, 'What am I supposed to be doing?' That much should go without saying. The habits of a good classroom should answer, 'You should be doing the do now, because we always start with the do now.'

Most types of questioning techniques and methods of quizzing can be used as a 'do now' task to ensure a prompt and focused start to the lesson. The do now supports the concept of starting lessons with regular retrieval practice and the style of the 'do now' task lends itself well to self-assessment. If pupils are completing a quiz or answering short answer questions, the teacher can present the correct answers to the class for the pupils to self-check and assess.

Peer assessment can also be used for a 'do now' task, but as mentioned previously, if this is used as an opportunity to promote retrieval practice then it is important to keep the stakes low. Peer assessment should be monitored by the teacher, so that before progressing to new material the teacher can gather an understanding of the pupils' levels of understanding or recall, and where any misconceptions may be lingering or common mistakes are being made.

On page 160 is an example of a 'do now' task in a KS3 lesson (Boxer, 2014). Once time has been provided to answer the questions (they can be presented to pupils via a paper quiz, digital tool or simply projected onto the board), pupils will be able to self-assess, check and, if necessary, correct their answers while being guided and monitored by the teacher.

'Do now' activity: Answer the questions below

Q1. What is a fuel?

Q2. What unit do we use to measure energy?

Q3. What is an energy store?

Q4. Which energy store is involved in fuels, food and batteries?

Q5. Which energy store is involved when objects heat up or cool down?

Q6. How is energy moved between energy stores?

Q7. What is the law of conservation of energy?

Q8. Which energy transfer is often involved in changing the temperature of objects?

'Do now' activity: Check your answers

Q1. What is a fuel? A substance that releases stored energy when it is burned.

Q2. What unit do we use to measure energy? Joules (J).

Q3. What is an energy store? When energy is held by an object for a time.

Q4. Which energy store is involved in fuels, food and batteries? Chemical energy store.

Q5. Which energy store is involved when objects heat up or cool down? Thermal energy store.

Q6. How is energy moved between energy stores? By energy transfer.

Q7. What is the law of conservation of energy? Energy cannot be created or destroyed.

Q8. Which energy transfer is often involved in changing the temperature of objects? Transfer from hot to cold.

When there is a lot of curriculum content to teach, it can be tempting to rush through self-assessment by instructing pupils to check if their answers are correct before quickly moving on. It is important that each question and answer is discussed; some may be covered briefly, whereas other questions may require further explanation and discussion. If the teacher is struggling for time then the number of questions asked in the 'do now' activity can be reduced, allowing more time for meaningful feedback and reflection.

Providing the answers for pupils is an example of clear feedback, but it is still important to support pupils. If they answered a question incorrectly, do they know why they were wrong? Do they now understand why the correct answer is accurate? This type of feedback is immediate, but as the lesson progresses it does not tend to be actionable feedback. The way pupils can act on the feedback provided is by answering the same questions at a later date, either as a retrieval practice task or homework quiz, with the aim that they will answer correctly next time.

Reflection tickets

Another way to encourage pupils to engage with feedback that goes beyond the score or grade is a reflection ticket. These tickets can be completed after a quiz that checks for understanding or after a retrieval quiz. The reflection ticket can be completed on paper, in class books or digitally.

The reflection ticket task encourages pupils to reflect on their scores and progress. Pupils can review their success and ability to correctly understand or recall information, and by identifying gaps in their knowledge they develop an awareness of the errors or gaps in their knowledge. This task is also useful for the teacher. I often skim read the tickets and made a note of common mistakes and shared gaps in knowledge, and I would then use this information to support my lesson planning and ensure I revisited the content with the class in order to close the knowledge gaps.

The example on page 162 shows a pupil reflecting on their areas of strength, the information they have understood and can recall, as well as recognising (through the feedback provided) their areas for improvement. They also reflect on the information they haven't grasped or that they forgot.

Reflection ticket

Areas of strength (accuracy and confidence)	Areas for improvement (gaps in knowledge)
• I remembered lots of correct information about the Buddha, Siddhartha Gautama – known as 'the enlightened one'. • I can confidently explain the Four Noble Truths and the beliefs about suffering in Buddhism. • I can explain in detail the concept of reincarnation and what followers of Buddhism believe about this. • I know the key words mantra, enlightenment, annata and annica and what they mean.	• I forgot what the Five Precepts are. I need to check my knowledge organiser because I have forgotten this twice. I know some of them but not all of them. • I wasn't able to answer the questions about the Buddhist temple. I was absent when this was taught in the lesson so I need to read the class notes Miss gave me. • I forgot what the 'Middle Way' meant but I now know this and when we do the quiz next time I think I will get this right!

Success criteria

Learning intentions are descriptions of the intended change in long-term capability, and they communicate to the class what they will be learning about in the short term (either in a lesson or series of lessons). Success criteria are descriptions of the desired performance in learning tasks. Learning intentions and success criteria differ in terms of what they refer to; the distinction is important because learning is a change in long-term memory, therefore learning cannot be judged in the moment.

Success criteria involve the manageable breakdown of the learning intentions to help the student achieve the desired goal in terms of content, skills and knowledge that needs to be learned. The learning intentions and success criteria must be explicitly linked, and the pupils should know and be aware of this too. Success criteria can be used as part of peer or self-assessment, and for teacher feedback. They can allow learners to monitor their own progress and assess their success, and can also show pupils explicitly what success looks like and what they are required to know or do.

Success criteria can be used for writing-based tasks to act as a reminder for pupils about basic literacy skills, or the criteria could be more subject specific. The criteria should be shared with pupils, where possible, for them to refer to during different stages of the learning process, encouraging independence and reflection with ongoing self-checking and correcting.

It is important that success criteria do not become a checklist that pupils don't engage with. Success criteria should support learners to make progress and understand how to be successful.

Read and relect, check and correct

A common experience for any teacher is when some students understand concepts before their peers do. There will also be times when pupils complete tasks and classwork before their classmates. This can pose a problem for the teacher, as they don't want to rush or put pressure on other learners to complete the task, understanding they need longer, while also making sure the pupils that have successfully completed tasks aren't waiting around with nothing else to do.

I previously used a 'challenge jar' that sat on my classroom desk. This jar would contain a range of generic extension activities for pupils to work on if they had completed their work and others were still working on a task. An example of this could be, 'Tell me three things from the lesson today you found interesting.'

My classes loved the challenge jar, but I quickly realised it was a bad idea. Pupils enjoyed completing work and selecting an extension task at random from the challenge jar, and the tasks were always designed to be fun and engaging. However, a problem with the tasks is that they did not provide enough challenge and were therefore only effective at keeping pupils busy.

Another problem I noticed with the challenge jar is that pupils had started to rush their classwork so they could go up to the desk and pick an extension task from the jar. This meant the quality of their classwork suffered and lots of mistakes were made. I knew the challenge jar had to go! I wanted to provide a meaningful extension task while also ensuring the quality of pupils' classwork improved.

I created the resource on page 164, which I entitled 'read and reflect, check and correct'. This resource can be used for peer or self-assessment.

The purpose of this task is to give the pupils specific instructions when reading through and reflecting on their classwork.

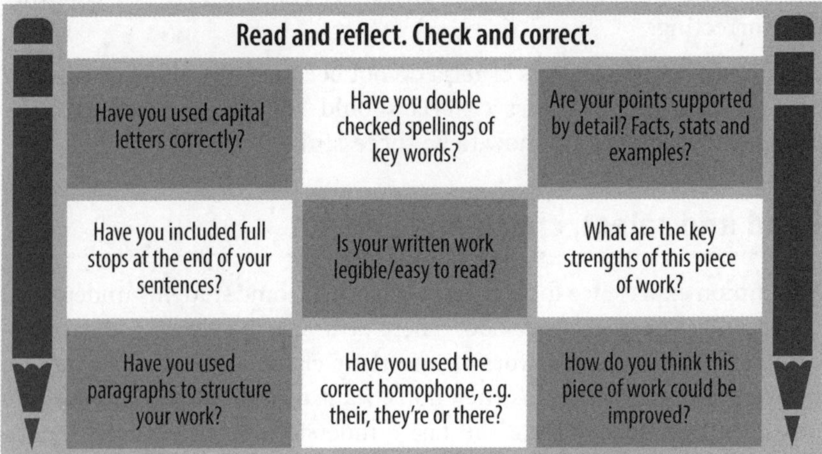

It is frustrating when pupils forget to use full stops when they already know sentences finish with them. This resource acts as a checklist for learners to make corrections and improve the quality of their written work before submitting it to me.

The pupils and I were able to quickly see a visible impact through the improvements they were making. Each pupil was given a copy of the resource to be glued in their books. A digital version was also made available online on the Google Classroom, and sometimes I would project it onto the class board as a visual reminder. The prompts can be added to a bookmark template that pupils can easily access when needed.

This example has a focus on literacy and was designed for pupils across KS3. The resource can be adapted for younger or older students, with more focus on subject specific elements or exam question requirements.

Knowledge organisers

Knowledge organisers were originally created by teacher and senior leader Joe Kirby (2015) for use at secondary level, with a focus on exam content and revision. A knowledge organiser is a document that contains the essential information covering a topic or unit. Kirby explains:

> A knowledge curriculum specifies, in meticulous detail, the exact facts, dates, events, characters, concepts and precise definitions that pupils are expected to master in long term memory. [...] The most powerful tool in the arsenal of the curriculum designer is the knowledge organiser. These organise all the most vital, useful and powerful knowledge on a single page.

Teachers can create their own knowledge organiser or use pre-made organisers that are available, but it is vital that the contents of the knowledge organiser are consistent with the curriculum content. The knowledge organiser should explicitly show learners (and parents) the specific knowledge they are required to understand and learn. An organiser is not a curriculum or scheme of work, but those documents can inspire and inform the creation and implementation of a knowledge organiser.

The following is an example of a knowledge organiser used in Year 5 geography, created by teacher and leader Adam Woodward.

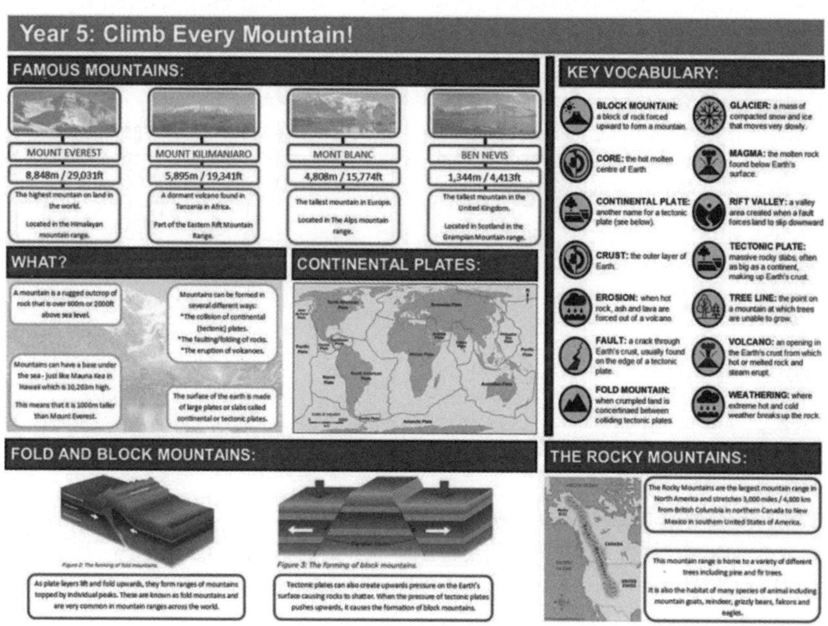

Pupils can use their knowledge organiser inside or outside of the classroom (this will depend on age). Organisers can be used throughout the learning process or for retrieval practice (with paired quizzing, for example) or act as the basis for creating flashcards. They can also be used to support parents by providing an overview of the content their child is expected to know, and parents can use a knowledge organiser to quiz their child as the information in the organiser will provide the answers.

Another way a knowledge organiser can be used (both inside and outside of the lesson) is for self-assessment and reflection. A pupil can use a knowledge organiser to create questions for self-quizzing; they can write down their answers and use the knowledge organiser to check for accuracy. Another method is for a pupil to write everything they can about a topic (alternatively, this can be done verbally either through self-recording or talking to a peer, friend or family member) and use the knowledge organiser to check for accuracy and discover any gaps in knowledge.

An example of self-assessment is shown in the following template.

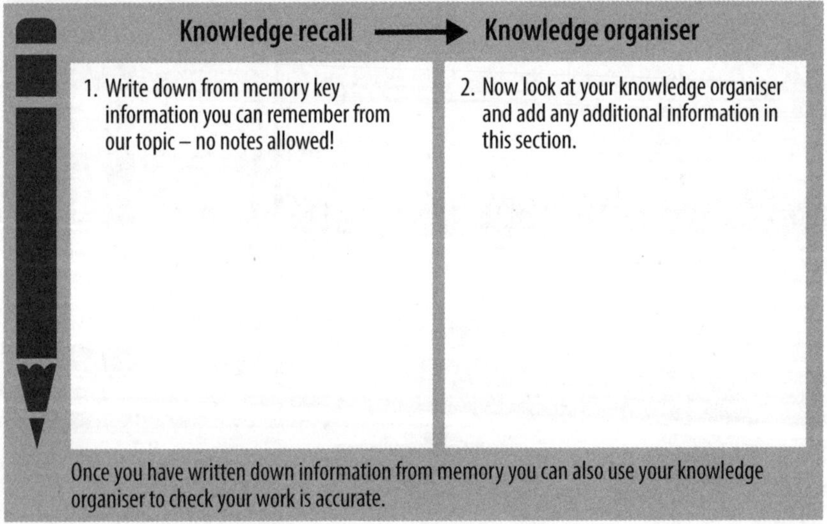

The following template shows generic questions that are linked to the knowledge organiser (the questions can be adapted to suit age and context). Once again, pupils can use their knowledge organiser to self-assess their answers.

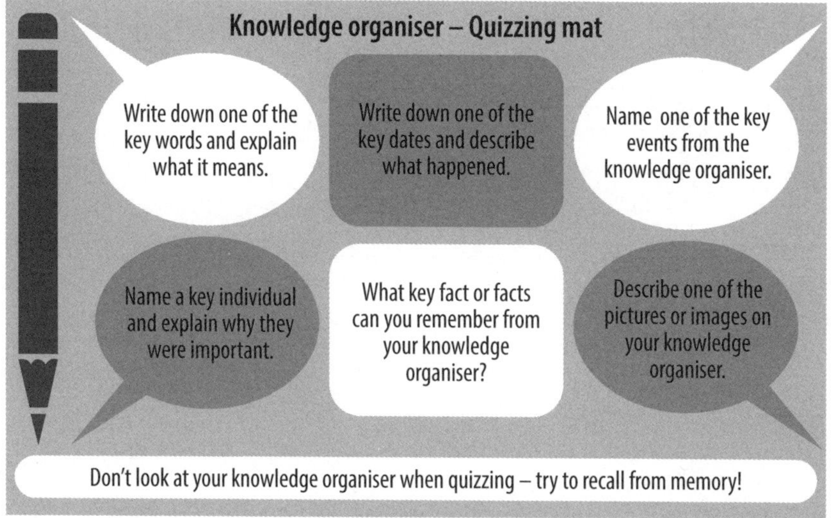

If the teacher creates their own knowledge organiser, for example using a PowerPoint slide format, it can be duplicated with certain sections of the organiser removed, as shown in the example on page 168. The duplicated version can then be used as a 'fill in the blanks' task for pupils to complete. Once they have filled in the blank spaces on the knowledge organiser, pupils can refer back to the original version to self-assess, check and correct their answers.

Knowledge organiser – Plants

Parts of a plant	Life cycle of a plant	What do plants need to grow?
		1. Water 2. 3. 4. 5.

Vocabulary

Roots	[Term]	Nutrients
[Definition]	Make food for the plant using carbon dioxide from the air and sunlight.	[Definition]

In summary, a knowledge organiser is essentially a feedback sheet for learners, as it contains all the answers and information pupils are required to know.

Flashcards

I am a passionate advocate of flashcards as an effective study strategy. My mantra to my classes, when explaining how to create and use flashcards, has been 'flashcards don't need to be flashy!' A flashcard should contain a question on one side and the correct answer on the flip side; alternatively, a key term can appear on the flashcard with the definition on the reverse, or they can be used for direct translations in language subjects.

Flashcards can be used inside or outside of a lesson to support learning, from consolidating knowledge to providing an opportunity to recall answers from long-term memory with retrieval practice. They are a learning resource that can be used with classmates, friends or family members or used independently. Anyone can ask the question on the flashcard without having prior knowledge of the topic or term, because the answer is on the other side of the card. Flashcards provide the learner with immediate feedback.

Again, as with any classroom technique or strategy, flashcards can be used effectively or ineffectively. It is essential for learners to understand how to create and use flashcards properly. The effectiveness of flashcards depends on how they are used, when they are used and what is included on the flashcards.

Pupils have to actually answer the question on the flashcard. This can be done through writing answers before checking the accuracy or answering verbally. Simply looking at a flashcard and then flipping it over is a wasted learning opportunity, meaning pupils have to be very self-disciplined. Pupils should place the cards in a pile based on their response – correct or incorrect. The incorrect pile will show the pupil the gaps in their knowledge and guide their future study.

I advise my pupils to stick to one question (or key term) per flashcard, as sorting the cards into organised piles – correct or incorrect – is much easier to do with one question. As an example, if a card contains three questions and the learner answers two right and one wrong, which pile should the card go into? It should go into the incorrect pile until all questions have been mastered, but keeping cards to a minimum of one question can help to keep the learner focused on knowledge gaps that need to be closed.

I initially promoted the use of flashcards with my older pupils, mainly in examination classes at GCSE and A level. I was sceptical about how effective flashcards could be with younger learners, as I viewed them as a retrieval revision aid in preparation for exams. I was wrong. Flashcards have the potential to be used with younger learners through to adult learners.

I have observed pupils in Year 1 using flashcards to practise and rehearse key words. The flashcards were used in a variety of ways in Year 1 (such as pair quizzing and self-quizzing), and learners were encouraged to spend time each week with their parents using their flashcards. The pupils must understand the feedback provided with the flashcard, or the task has the potential to cause confusion and waste precious learning time.

There are various websites and apps, such as Carousel, Quizlet, Quizizz and Anki, that enable users to create their own flashcards or use pre-made versions. They also provide the pupil with immediate feedback, and some digital tools and websites will store the data and record the feedback for the learner.

Flashcards shouldn't be used as a method of intense last-minute cramming before an exam. A key reason for this is the feedback that flashcard quizzing can generate. If, for example, a learner is using flashcards to recall information from long-term memory and the flashcards have highlighted gaps in knowledge, the pupil will need time to close those knowledge gaps. If a learner is using flashcards the evening before an assessment or exam and gaps have been identified, there is a limited amount of time to do anything about it, which could add pressure and stress.

Exam wrappers

'Exam wrappers', originally credited to Marsha Lovett (Kaplan et al, 2013) were designed as a self-reflection resource for learners after they have completed an assessment or exam. As discussed previously, it can be tempting for learners to focus on scores and grades, but they need to engage with the feedback provided and reflect to help them learn and continue to progress.

The exam wrappers encourage pupils to reflect, openly and honestly, on their effort, preparation prior to the exam and methods of revision. If the pupil did spend a lot of time revising and they were disappointed in their overall result, the exam wrapper might help the teacher and learner to identify the problem.

An example could be that the pupil spent hours studying, but most of this time was spent cramming the night before the exam by re-reading notes. In this case, the teacher can advise the pupil to use spaced retrieval practice in the future. Exam wrappers focus on the process, as well as the final result.

The wrapper can then go on to explore different questions, breaking down the time spent and marks awarded. This enables a deep dive that helps the learner to fully understand their areas of strength and weakness and inform their next steps. Alex Quigley (2018) writes about exam wrappers:

> This helpful feedback strategy, labelled 'exam wrappers' because they wrap around information on how the student has revised, offers important information for the teacher to help diagnose how effective, or extensive (or not), revision has proven. Also, it can prove a good way to help puncture student over-confidence in their revision.

In addition to providing an opportunity for learners to reflect on their performance, the exam wrappers can provide insight and further understanding for the teacher, helping to shape future planning. I have seen various examples of exam wrappers online, where teachers have adapted the resource depending on the age, subject or focus of the exam.

The following is an example of a clear and concise exam wrapper from Louise Lewis, experienced biology teacher and research lead. Louise explains that pupils complete the first section (points 1–4) prior to the test or before they receive their results. Learners complete the second part (points 5–8) after they have received their marks and results.

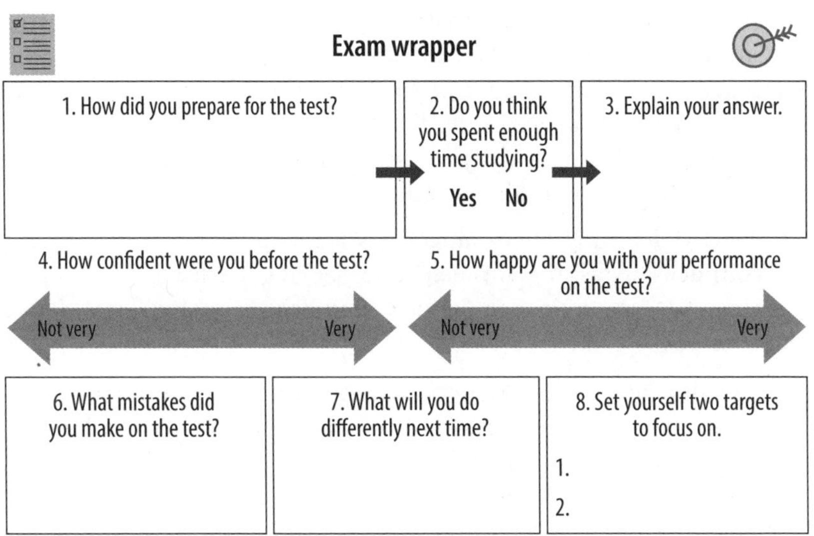

This example exam wrapper is generic and therefore has many advantages; it can be used by colleagues in the department and across other subjects. This template can also be used for different assessments and year groups. It is possible to create subject specific exam wrappers that break down the exam into different papers, units or questions. This can help the learner to recognise where to focus and direct their future revision.

The EEF 'Metacognition and Self-regulated Learning Guidance Report' (published in 2018 and updated in 2021) featured exam wrappers, stating:

> Teaching tools like 'exam wrappers' (a post-exam student self-evaluation feedback tool) offer teachers and pupils a way to evaluate and analyse errors, and revision patterns, for a given exam. This can help improve pupils' accuracy of judgement.

Encourage pupils to ask for help

We want children to be able to ask for support and seek feedback throughout the learning process. Asking for help is a sign of strength, not weakness, although for many children (and adults) it can be challenging or uncomfortable to recognise when help is needed. It can also be difficult to know where to find help.

In a school context it is vital that everyone can access help when they need it. This includes pupils, staff and members of the wider school community. Providing help can be done through various methods such as offering explanations, feedback, guidance, advice or assistance. Support is provided on a daily basis in a school environment and can range from pastoral to academic issues.

A supportive learning environment is where students feel comfortable and confident in asking for help and seeking feedback. The 'Great Teaching Toolkit: Evidence Review' published by Evidence Based Education (2020) states:

> Great teachers create a supportive environment for learning. [...] A supportive environment is characterised by relationships of trust and respect between students and teachers, and among students. It is one in which students are motivated, supported and challenged and have a positive attitude towards their learning.

It is important to ensure that any request for help is taken seriously and understand that some pupils may grasp new concepts and content at a different pace to their peers. The review goes on to advise:

> Teachers should convey care, empathy and warmth towards their students and avoid negative emotional behaviours, such as using sarcasm, shouting or humiliation.

Building a supportive environment where pupils feel they can ask questions and make mistakes can contribute to a culture where feedback is welcomed and embraced. But even if learners feel they can ask questions, this does not necessarily mean that they will.

Researchers Amanda Sebesta and Elena Bray Speth (2017) examined undergraduates in the United States and found that students who use strategies like asking for help are more likely to achieve the highest grades. This is a powerful finding, and one learners should be aware of.

High achieving students take ownership and responsibility for their learning and are able to ask for help, contributing to their successful grades. Pupils can be reluctant to ask for help or refuse to do so; this was also illustrated in Sebesta and Speth's study. The study found that only around 16% of undergraduate students ask their teachers or instructors for help, but of the students whose grade improved over the semester, over 97% sought assistance.

There are often signs when someone is struggling; these can be evident through certain behaviours, classwork and academic attainment. However, teachers, leaders, parents, carers or tutors may not realise that pupils need help. Furthermore, it is an aim for pupils to take control and ownership of their learning; this includes asking for help when needed. Pupils need to know when they need help, and teachers can provide opportunities and support to aid them in understanding this. Through setting tasks that are 'desirably difficult', providing actionable feedback and prompting critical reflections, teachers can help learners to recognise when to ask for assistance.

As teachers and leaders, it is an essential part of our job to help and support learners. We know that simply explaining curricular content does not necessarily equate with pupil learning, hence the importance of eliciting evidence of learning, asking questions and checking for understanding, which are all followed by providing feedback to learners.

Chapter summary

- Self-assessment is not easy. Pupils will require explicit guidance, support and monitoring. Some pupils may overestimate their achievements while others may underestimate theirs. Self-assessment should therefore not be used for summative assessment, but instead for formative assessment and continual reflection and self-regulation.
- There are tasks that lend themselves well to self-assessment, such as quizzing and 'do now' activities.
- The best person to mark a quiz is the person who has just taken it.
- Resources such as knowledge organisers and 'read and reflect, check and correct' can be used to help learners self-assess their work.

Chapter 5
Peer assessment

Peer assessment (or critique) is the process by which pupils provide feedback to one or more of their peers. It is another method of feedback that can be used alongside many other approaches. Peer assessment can be carried out verbally, through written comments or using technology. As with self-assessment, pupils should not be expected to carry out peer assessment blindly, without any clear instruction, guidance or support from the teacher or without access to assessment criteria or a mark scheme.

Paul Chin, head of learning and teaching at the Centre for Learning and Teaching at the University of Bath, published an article drawing on research that focused on peer assessment in education. Chin (2016) writes:

> There have been many decades of research into the potential benefits of peer assessment and numerous studies have shown that peer assessment offers real educational, and sometimes social, benefits for students.

Peer assessment provides pupils with the opportunity to review others' work and engage with the ideas, opinions and answers expressed by their peers. It also encourages learners to reflect on their peers' work, which in turn can support them to reflect on their own work by comparing and contrasting. Peer assessment also involves learners in the feedback and assessment process, potentially helping them to gain a further understanding of and appreciation for the feedback they receive.

A TES article (2019) explores the drawbacks of peer assessment (which will be covered later in this chapter), but also highlights some of the benefits of peer assessment:

> Peer assessment can help to secure and develop a pupil's understanding of how they are assessed and how particular marks and grades are awarded. By assessing others' work, they are able to critically reflect on tasks and evaluate their own learning while also exploring how their peers have approached and prepared their answer(s). [...] It can provide pupils with examples of good practice and therefore model how an answer might be formed or might look. If combined with more formal teacher assessment, peer assessment can provide students with instant feedback and help to reduce the teacher's marking load.

The Teaching and Learning Innovation Centre (TaLIC) at the University of Hong Kong (Chan, 2010) describes the advantages of peer assessment, noting:

> It can be extremely valuable in helping students to learn from each other by listening, analysing and problem solving. It gives students the opportunity to encounter diversity in different ways, critique and judge and ultimately, students learn how to be responsible for their own learning.

Nancy Falchikov and Judy Goldfinch (2000) published a meta-analysis focusing on peer assessment that compares peer and teacher marks (although this is in the context of higher education). The authors explain that when peer assessment is designed well it can be considered as a reliable and valid method of assessment. The abstract states that 'studies with high design quality appear to be associated with more valid peer assessments than those which have poor experimental design.'

Several studies have investigated pupil perceptions of fairness in peer assessment (many papers focus on students in a university context, as this approach is increasingly being used in higher education). A study published in 2023 (Carvalho) describes the experiences of peer assessment in a problem-based course at a Portuguese university, involving 120 students across seven semesters. This study brought to light that students can have 'significantly different experiences of peer assessment, but also in their experiences of teamwork.' The results revealed:

> Although the larger cluster (70%) expressed a positive experience, the other group perceived peer assessment results and final marks to be unfair and reported incidents of friendship-marking and conflict arising from peer assessment. Results show that perceptions of fairness (both regarding peer assessment and final marks) are very much associated with those problems.

The conditions for the study are different from peer assessment in a classroom environment, but some interesting points were raised. According to the report, 29% of students admitted to 'friendship-marking', 34% of learners reported there was conflict associated with peer assessment and over a quarter of students (27%) strongly agreed it was hard to assess their classmates. These issues can occur and be a problem in a classroom environment.

It is worth stressing that peer assessment should only be used to provide formative feedback to help learners improve, and not provide an overall grade, judgement or high stakes evaluation. The meta-analysis in Portugal did review peer assessment in the context of both formative and summative assessment, and shows that reducing the stakes of peer assessment can remove concerns about fairness and accuracy with formal summative assessments.

Dylan Wiliam and Siobhan Leahy (2015) clearly express their stance on peer assessment by writing, 'It is quite wrong for one student to be placed in the position of evaluating the achievement of another student for the purpose of reporting to parents or others.' It is important that pupils are explicitly told this before they assess their peers' work.

A study by Stonewall, Dorneich and Rongerude, published in 2024, focused on 'training to increase student perceptions of fairness in peer assessment.' Once again, this was in the context of higher education. The peer assessment training offered to students was designed to 'address fairness in higher education group learning', when students were collaborating and working as teams. The report illustrates once again that pupil perception of peer assessment can be negative, showing that 'students often view the peer assessment process as unfair due to the potential for biased ratings or perceived lack of peer qualification.'

The findings of the study revealed the following:

> Results indicated that students had higher perceptions of fairness in their peer assessments after training. Students were also more confident in theirs and their peers' fair rating skills. These results indicate that classroom training could be used to increase peer assessment fairness. Fairer peer assessment provides enhanced access to active and team learning benefits to a broader range of students, potentially impacting the retention of a more diverse population of practitioners in the field.

Although the focus in this study was higher education, the implications of the findings can translate to the school classroom. Training pupils to be able to provide peer feedback that is fair, reliable, understandable, helpful and actionable is essential. There are various ways the teacher can train learners, including providing examples, modelling and through regular monitoring and support.

The following are potential problems with peer assessment.

- **Pupils can struggle to give each other effective feedback.** The feedback they give to their classmates could be inaccurate, unhelpful or even hurtful. Understanding of the task and success criteria is vital.
- **Peer assessment takes time.** It takes time to model and show learners how to provide feedback, as well as for the teacher to discuss the success or assessment criteria. It also takes time for peers to review the work and then provide feedback, and for pupils to act on this feedback.
- **Pupils don't always value peer assessment.** The teacher is the expert in the room, and therefore pupils might prefer or expect feedback from them rather than the person sitting next to them.
- **Peer assessment can be difficult for the teacher to monitor.** In a large class it can be a challenge for the teacher to check and oversee the peer assessment and feedback conversations or comments for all learners.
- **Relationships can impact and influence the feedback provided.** Pupils may be tempted to give generous feedback to their friends or perhaps very critical comments to individuals they view as

competition. Learners may be biased, though peer feedback can be carried out anonymously if necessary. Some pupils may be reluctant to offer feedback to their peers because they feel uncomfortable or lack the confidence to do so.

- **It can be especially challenging for learners with SEND or EAL.** These pupils may lack the skills, understanding or confidence to carry out peer assessment.

The negative reputation peer assessment has in education was explored by author Alex Quigley, writing in the TES (2024), when he asked the question, 'Why is peer feedback and assessment so commonly relegated to the margins of teaching practice?' Quigley, an advocate for peer assessment in the classroom, explains:

> Done well, it can move learning forward, make pupils more responsive to feedback, and it can potentially reduce teacher workload. Though it is no doubt tricky to get right in the classroom, the benefits of peer assessment can be worth the effort.

The challenges with peer assessment can be overcome through careful planning, clear instruction and regular monitoring and support. Once again the key feedback principles apply – feedback provided to learners should be understandable, helpful and actionable.

Peer scoring

Although self-assessment has been described as the best method for marking quizzes by Dylan Wiliam (2017), an alternative is peer scoring. This type of feedback can be used for spelling tests, definitions or quizzing to check for understanding or long-term recall. This type of feedback lends itself well to peer scoring because there is not much room for the peer to deviate in terms of the feedback they provide; it can be clear and concrete with correct or incorrect. There is no room for bias or 'friendship scoring'.

However, a word of caution is to take care when using peer scoring in the classroom. Pupils with SEND may find the concept of their peer checking their answers and providing a score to be quite daunting. As stated previously, a retrieval task should be low stakes, but peer scoring may create a high stakes atmosphere. Pupils may be embarrassed if they lack confidence or have struggled with the quiz. They may not want their peers to know their scores, and this could make them anxious.

A teacher can work hard to create a classroom culture where there is supportive and kind learning, but it can be a challenge. The same challenges faced by students with SEND could also apply to students with EAL, although this will not always be an issue. Knowledge of pupils is key to making judgements and decisions about whether or not it is appropriate to use peer assessment for quizzing.

Highlighter hints

The 'highlighter hints' approach is very similar to dot marking (discussed in chapter 4), but it provides the learner with more support and guidance. Instead of placing a dot in the margin for the pupil to find and fix the error on that line, the teacher or peer will use a highlighter pen to identify specifically where the error is.

If the teacher is using this approach, it can take place live during a lesson, which is preferable as the pupil can immediately act on the feedback and rectify the mistake. However, it can also take place outside of a lesson if a teacher is reviewing classwork. This approach is considerably quicker than providing written comments.

The highlighter hints method works well for peer assessment as it enables learners to assess the work of their peers and highlight any errors. When the pupil receives their work, they must act on the highlighted sections by correcting the error. The following is an example of pupil classwork that has been highlighted by their peer – literacy and factual errors have been highlighted. The pupil has a responsibility to address and rectify the highlighted errors.

> World War One began in 1912 and ended in 1918. There were several causes of the war. These causes included militaryism, the alliances, imperialism, nationalism and the asasination of Franz Ferdinand. I believe all the causes of the war were significant, but some played a more important role than others. In my opinion the main cause of WW1 was the death of Franz Ferdinand, as this is the event that caused anger and outrage, it encouraged countries to fight.

Different coloured highlighter pens can be used for different errors; for example, any spelling errors could be identified in one colour and factual errors in a different colour, though this can lead to overcomplicating a simple approach to feedback and corrections.

Kind, specific, helpful

The 'kind, specific and helpful' approach has become widely used in schools. This concept is taken from the work of author Ron Berger, specifically his book, *An Ethic of Excellence: Building a Culture of Craftsmanship with Students* (2003), and has become well known and regarded in education.

Berger identifies three key elements that are essential for effective peer assessment and critique.

Kind

Kindness is key in any school environment, and receiving feedback can be very personal and emotive. It is important that while feedback is honest it is always communicated in a way that is not personal, mocking or cruel but instead thoughtful and considerate.

I have read many examples of feedback where pupils have written or said things to one another such as 'your handwriting is awful, I can't read it!' This can be very upsetting and damaging for students' confidence and motivation. As adults, whenever we are giving feedback we should also take care to be kind.

Specific

The need for detail and precision can be very difficult for pupils to grasp. If literacy targets are vague and generalised ('improve punctuation', for example), this may not be helpful; instead, the feedback needs to be focused and specific (such as 'always use full stops at the end of sentences') in order to have an impact on pupils' progress. Teachers should model examples of this in their feedback and when instructing pupils as to how to provide peer feedback.

Helpful

Ultimately, all feedback should be helpful with formative assessment, otherwise what is the point in receiving the feedback? The more specific the feedback is, the more helpful it can be.

Receiving peer feedback

Being able to provide feedback and critique that is kind, specific and helpful is important, but if that feedback is ignored by the pupil receiving it then it has been a waste of precious lesson time. How learners react to, respond to and act on the critique and feedback provided is essential to ensuring peer feedback is effective.

The following example stresses the importance of learners being able to receive feedback from their peers.

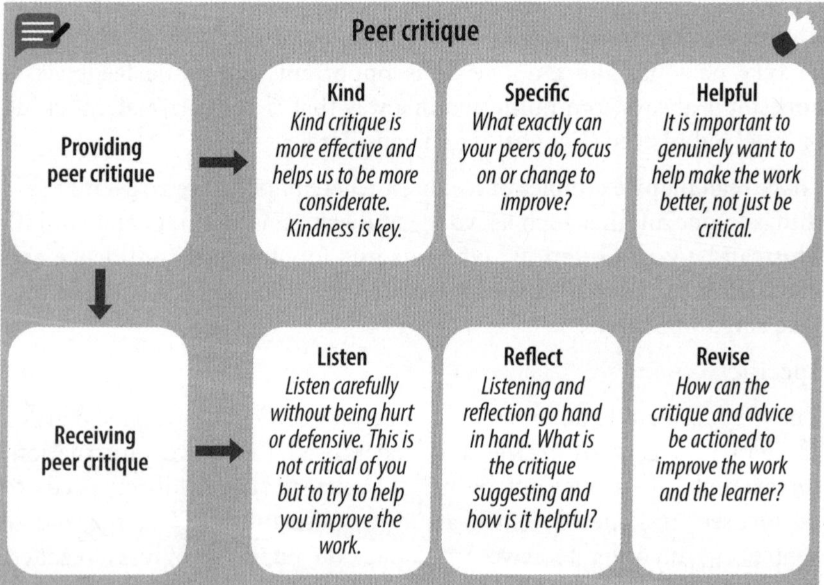

I collaborated with Ron Berger to identify three key points in helping learners receive peer critique. This guidance about receiving peer critique is to encourage pupils to embrace rather than dismiss or ignore critique from their classmates.

Listen

Listening has to be the first part of the process when receiving critique and feedback. As John Hattie (Chiles, 2020) asks, 'If feedback falls in a classroom and no one hears it, did it make a sound?' Listening is absolutely essential in a classroom, whether that be the student listening to the teacher, the teacher listening to their students or peers listening to each other.

The main aim of peer critique is for pupils to support and learn from one another, but this cannot be achieved if they don't listen to the peer feedback they receive. Note that this principle only applies if the feedback is verbal; if pupils provide each other with written feedback, 'listen' changes to 'read'.

Pupils may not value or respect feedback from their peers as much as they do from their teachers. This is understandable, as the teacher is the expert in the room. Despite this, pupils need to recognise that they can learn from peer critique and improve as a result. Peer critique must not be ignored.

Reflect

Teachers recognise the power of reflection, as this is something we constantly encourage to improve and develop our practice. Pupils also need to understand the power of reflection.

Listening and reflection go hand in hand. Listening without reflection is more akin to hearing critique rather than understanding and responding to it. Do pupils actually know how to reflect on their work and any critique provided? As teachers, we need to model this and have explicit conversations about what reflection looks like and how it can have a positive impact, helping pupils to move forward with their progress.

Revise

The final element is to revise their original piece of work, which is why peer feedback should be actionable. Once pupils have listened to and reflected on the critique, they will know how to act on it. If the critique has been kind, specific and helpful, this will improve pupils' chances of using the critique to improve their work as well as applying that feedback to future tasks and performance.

Case study: Promoting powerful peer assessment

Bio: Martin Ferguson is head of English at Ashfield Girls' High School, Belfast, and a member of the school's teaching, learning and assessment team. In 2023, he published his first book, *See One, Do One, Teach One: 12 lessons to support GCSE English*.

Peer assessment has had a bad reputation over the years because of the conflation between summative and formative peer assessment, and what that might look like in the classroom. As Dylan Wiliam (2017) rightly stated, 'a lot of people just assume we are talking about having kids marking each other's work so that the teacher doesn't have to do it.' With careful structuring and modelling of the peer assessment process, formative peer assessment or tutoring encourages self-reflection and can help pupils help each other to improve their work.

The process also allows for the internalising of success criteria and a greater understanding of tasks and their component parts, for example extended writing or writing for a specific purpose. Peer assessment enriches classroom discussion, encourages and assists high quality feedback and fosters metacognition as part of the classroom culture.

In order to effectively embed this practice in my own lessons, I created a flow chart that I use and share with the class to ensure structure and clarity. The flow chart helps to demystify the process and makes it scalable across other departments. With peer assessment, pupils can independently identify how to move their learning forward, and when this is done in unison with responsive teaching and guidance in the classroom, the effect can be very powerful.

The overarching aim and culture that you want to create is 'progression over perfection', which, having worked in an all-girls' school for six years, has helped to shift some mindsets and fostered an 'attempt it first and fix it later' approach. It normalises mistakes and develops good working relationships and teacher–pupil trust. This also encourages risk taking in their writing; for example, I noticed when I referred to enhancing or extending vocabulary in their writing (because pupils had been using a thesaurus in order to set their work apart from others), this enriched classroom discussions and created a climate of independence and ownership. We then had further discussions about choice of vocabulary and using it in the correct context.

In my book, *See One, Do One, Teach One*, I used scripted feedback questions that can be used to structure the 'teach one' part of the lesson (see an example on page 186). This has proven to be invaluable because often when teachers let go of the reins and ask pupils to partake in classroom discussion, the lesson and focus can become blurred, or momentum can be lost. However, if we structure our talk with the same rigour that we would structure a written piece or the content and delivery of a lesson, the result is very powerful as pupils remain on task while partaking in meaningful, rich talk.

Teachers can also use scripted feedback as a series of questions for whole class discussion, recap or plenary. Successful peer assessment, like most lessons in teaching, is really down to setting it up for success and careful planning. Once the process is commonplace in the classroom, then the pupils – and the teacher – will fall into the rhythm of using it.

Structuring and nurturing 'rich talk' in the classroom

Examiner: **Grade:**

GCSE English language	Unit 4: Personal and creative writing		
Writing checklist	**Writing targets**		
Opening and impact: Have they...	**Met**	**Working towards**	**Not met**
included a lively and engaging opening or introduction?			
included language techniques in their opening?			
included an exclamatory statement, rule of three or rhetorical question in their opening?			
List any techniques they have used in the opening below:			
used ambitious or strong vocabulary to impress the examiner in the opening paragraphs?			
used a style that suits the audience and purpose?			
Structure, vocabulary and punctuation: Have they...			
used accurate spelling of regular words?			
used adverbs (-ly words) to describe the action?			
used a range of short and long sentences?			
used a range of punctuation for effect? . , ? . . . ! ()			
used paragraphs properly or where appropriate?			
Content, style and ending: Have they...			
managed to keep the reader's interest?			
included an anecdote (own experiences) in their writing?			
included any language techniques for an effective ending?			
included a strong ending with a final thought or message?			

What do you think this pupil could do in order to improve their writing?

____

____

____

____

____

Grade %:

A	80+
B	73+
C*	68–72
C	60+
D	50+

Top tip: If you have success criteria for specific tasks, you can laminate them and give them out with a whiteboard and pen. Pupils can add their own criteria and can tick off the parts that the tutee has included in their writing. This can be reused and saves time.

The resources I use are also time savers as they are explicitly connected to the core objectives of the task or mark scheme or are prepared beforehand with opportunities for pupils to feed into them. There is really no point in doing all of this without effective feedback from the teacher to close the feedback loop, so we use PDFs that can be 'tabbed' in order to complete them and are reusable. This means the cognitive load is off the pupil as they do not have to write it down and the feedback is uniform and familiar in KS3.

Feedback frames

Feedback frames can be very helpful for pupils when focusing on kind, specific and helpful peer feedback. The following example has been shared by Durrington High School on their teaching and learning blog.

Kind

- I really like the way you ______
- Excellent ______ throughout
- The most successful thing about this was ______
- I enjoyed reading this because ______
- It was especially good when you ______

Specific

- In the first/second/third analytical paragraph…
- I think your ______ is quite difficult to understand/could be explained better/could include more detail
- Add more detail to your ______
- Your point/analysis about ______ was ______ because ______

Helpful (refer to success criteria)

- Think about adding a ______
- Don't forget you need to ______
- Have you thought about ______
- To improve your ______ try ______
- Perhaps you could ______

A feedback frame can be adapted for different key stages and subjects to further support learners, and it can also include subject specific examples. The feedback frames can be used to support peer feedback with written comments or verbally. Learners with SEND or EAL can use the feedback frames as prompts and general guidance when giving feedback to their peers.

TAG Me!

Many educators use the TAG Me scaffolded approach to structure peer feedback (more commonly with younger pupils at primary and KS3), and the method has also gained popularity online. TAG Me is made up of the following stages:

- Tell me something you like (about my work).
- Ask me a question (based on my work).
- Give me a suggestion (to improve my work).

The first stage – 'Tell me something you like' – is to encourage learners to provide praise to their peers. This is often easy for pupils to do, but they must not give vague statements such as 'I like your story', as they need to be more specific. They may like a character in the short story, or perhaps they like a twist in the plot. Pupils may also like specific ideas or an approach their classmate has taken.

'Ask me a question' can be an opportunity for a pupil to probe further and find out more, asking questions to encourage their partner to explain further and expand on their original points or answer. The question should be thoughtful and linked to the learning material and classwork. If the pupil is confused about an aspect of the classwork, their question can address this. The question could be about why they have reached an answer or made a decision to do something in a certain way in their work.

The final stage – 'Give me a suggestion' – is the part of the peer assessment that should be actionable. The suggestion should be clear about how to improve and should have an instruction or guidance as to how their peer can develop their work. This should help the learner understand what their next steps are.

The teacher should model examples of TAG Me peer feedback so learners can see for themselves what a good example looks like – and possibly a bad example too! TAG Me can also be supported by feedback frames (as shown in the previous example) or with sentence starters and examples to give the learners some guidance.

TAG Me can combine written and verbal peer feedback. It is a good idea for pupils to write down their feedback for each point so they don't forget, but they can elaborate on their written feedback by talking it through with their partner. TAG Me feedback can be carried out in a variety of ways, for example written on a sticky note attached to classwork or via a digital document that allows other users to collaborate and comment.

This peer feedback approach can be used with the person sitting next to the learner, pupils could be assigned a specific peer feedback partner, or they could be given an anonymous piece of work, so they don't know who in the class they are providing the feedback to.

Tracey Hare, a middle school art educator based in the US, instructs her pupils to write TAG down the left side of a sticky note (2015). The class places their in-progress artwork on their workspaces and then leave their seats. Music is played as learners walk around the class and view the artwork by their peers. When the music stops the learners should sit next to the artwork closest to them (not their own work) and after reviewing the artwork in front of them, they complete the TAG Me on the sticky note, before sticking it on the work for the individual to read once when they return to their seat.

Think, pair, share

Think, pair, share is a popular classroom technique, but it is not often associated with feedback despite it being a central feature of the method. Think, pair, share is more commonly associated with questioning, checking for understanding and promoting opportunities for debate, discussion and collaboration in the classroom, but it can and should be used as a way for learners to provide one another with feedback.

Using think, pair, share, the teacher will ask a question, provide a statement or pose a problem for the class to solve. Individuals have time during the 'think' stage to consider their initial response. I co-authored an article with Dylan Wiliam (2021), in which we provided advice to teachers to support getting the think, pair, share technique right, pointing out:

> One of the biggest challenges in implementing think, pair, share is making sure to not skimp on the think. When you pose a question to your class, the first impulse for students will be to turn and talk to a peer, skipping the thinking stage. Ensuring that ample 'think time' is provided before the pair and shared steps take place can prevent this impulse. [...] Think time prepares students so that

when they do talk to their partner, they have something to share, potentially adding another factor: think, pair, compare and share.

After the initial stage and thinking time, pupils can turn to their partner to discuss their answer. This is where pupils can provide feedback to one another. As discussed, a key aspect of engaging with feedback is listening. With this in mind, Wiliam and I offer advice to teachers:

> Make certain that during the pair and share stages students listen attentively to their talk partners. Students can be tagged 'A' and 'B' (for example, by the alphabetical order of their names), so that when the teacher tells the 'A' students to talk, 'B' students listen and then switch. A particularly powerful way of making students accountable for listening to their peers is to make it clear that they are likely to be asked to report to the class what their partner said ('Emily, can you tell us what Sarah told you?').

Holding pupils to account is important as they may be tempted to discuss something not related to the lesson and use peer reviewing as an opportunity to chat socially. The focus needs to be on the feedback they are providing to each other. Throughout the discussions the pupils might find they are in agreement with their answers, and this can provide them with confirmation and confidence. They can also use these opportunities to combine their answers and develop their original response, and to add more depth or explanation (depending on the question or task).

However, pupils may have different answers or ideas, and this will also need to be discussed at the pair stage. They can correct or challenge one another; feedback provided by one peer might help their partner to realise a mistake they have made and recognise the correct answer as a result. At this second stage a teacher can be monitoring the discussions, to ensure the learners are focused and to gauge pupils' responses.

The final aspect of think, pair, share is to share responses with the whole class. This can be achieved in a variety of ways, including the use of mini whiteboards or cold calling. If using mini whiteboards, the teacher can quickly scan the class responses and provide immediate verbal feedback to the class. If using cold calling, they can ask a pupil to share their answer, giving the rest of the pupils some time to reflect and receive feedback from their partner, meaning they may be more willing and eager to share with the rest of the class. The teacher can ask further questions, for example asking if the pupils initially had the same answer or if their answers differed.

This is good practice for pupils to provide feedback to one another and receive informal verbal peer feedback. As with any classroom technique, the more pupils do this in the lesson the easier it can become, as it will become ingrained as a classroom norm.

Peer feedback with immediate impact

Most peer feedback on extended pieces of writing tends to take place once the task is completed, but this risks reducing the impact. In a lesson where an extended written task is taking place, the teacher often does not have the luxury to continually provide feedback to pupils after each paragraph – there are too many pupils and not enough time. However, this approach can be used as a form of peer assessment, with pupils regularly providing feedback to one another throughout the process, not at the end.

The following example demonstrates this in action; it is from one of my Year 7 classes writing an extended piece answering a key question, 'Why did William win the Battle of Hastings?' (With permission granted by the pupil and parents.)

The Saxon Gazette 22/11/23

Royal Rumble!

Sp Hastings

Quite recently, King Harold was slaughtered at Hastigs as the Saxons fought a tough battle against William the Wonderful and his army.

⊕ Good bias/ Alliteration

Ⓣ check key words
Ⓣ too short and not so detailed

= good
= fix it

in January / There

This all started when Edward the Confessor died since he did not have a heir to the throne their there was a fuss about who would be the next King of England. Apparently Harold was supposed to be King since the late Edward promised him the throne. But everyone knows William the Wonderful should be King!

Only the first paragraph has been peer assessed, as this is what I instructed the class to do. An important aspect of formative assessment is that it is happening during the learning process and not simply bolted on at the end once a task is completed.

The pupil providing feedback has identified that their peer has incorrectly spelt the key term Hastings – writing 'Hastigs' – and they have used the literacy code 'SP' to identify this. The fact that this has been highlighted (using the helpful highlights approach) means that for the rest of the essay the pupil will now be aware of how to spell Hastings correctly. This is very clear feedback that the learner understood; it was helpful, and they were able to act on it.

If the peer assessment had taken place once the essay was completed, it is likely the pupil would have continued to spell the key term incorrectly throughout. This makes the approach very powerful, as it involves immediate feedback that the learner can respond to and appreciate.

The feedback provided by the pupil also encouraged more detail, and while this could be more specific, we can see the pupil receiving the feedback did make a conscious effort to include more detail in the second paragraph. Not only did the pupil improve their first paragraph, but they were able to continually improve with ongoing and regular feedback from their peer. I can recall the Year 7 pupil asking his partner, 'Can you look at this paragraph for me now?' This simple moment was wonderful to observe. The pupils were valuing the support and feedback they could give one another.

Another aspect of the peer feedback was the use of colour coding to highlight if the work was 'good' or the pupil needed to 'fix it'; this was the language chosen by the pupil. While there isn't anything wrong with 'what went well', 'even better if' and other similar phrases, they often don't reflect how pupils communicate to one another. I personally don't have a set of phrases that pupils must use when providing peer feedback, but I will provide guidance and prompts. As long as feedback is kind, specific and helpful, as well as understandable and actionable, then I am happy for the pupils to articulate this in a clear manner, but again this is a decision that comes under the remit of professional judgement and autonomy.

Peer sticky notes

Wiliam and Leahy (2015) offer useful advice about the use of sticky notes for both teacher and peer feedback, as an alternative to annotations on pupils' work. A sticky note can contain feedback and be stuck next to (or on top of) the relevant work being assessed.

Pupils can regard comments by others as a sign that their work is not good enough, or they could be unhappy that another person's writing has altered their piece or tarnished their presentation. To combat this, Wiliam and Leahy suggest that pupils write their peer feedback on sticky notes. If the recipient does not find the feedback helpful they can peel off the notes and discard them, or they can act on the feedback but not feel that their work has been tainted. Although we shouldn't encourage pupils to ignore peer feedback, there may be occasions when the feedback provided by the peer isn't helpful or accurate.

It can be very frustrating as a teacher when a pupil says their peer has spelled a key term incorrectly, when in fact they spelled it correctly in the first place! It is always worth emphasising the importance of peer feedback, but it does take time for students to grasp, so sticky notes are a great idea, especially in the early stages of embedding the strategy.

Sticky notes can be used with both the TAG Me approach and the next method, 'gallery critique'.

Gallery critique

The gallery critique idea is credited to Ron Berger (2003) as part of his extensive work to promote effective peer critique in the classroom. This activity is an extension of peer feedback as it involves all pupils in a class providing feedback on each other's work, again using Berger's key principles of being kind, specific and helpful.

There are a number of ways in which this can be trialled and implemented in the classroom, but the following is a general summary of the gallery critique approach:

- The classroom becomes a viewing gallery in which pupils' classwork is displayed or presented on tables for the rest of the class to view.

(Ensuring anonymity by removing names can avoid any potential biases such as friendship groups.) Berger recommends pupils view their peers' work in silence so they can carefully review and reflect.

- Pupils must be provided with sufficient time to review the different pieces of classwork. These could be a painting, illustration or model, an answer to an exam question or a section of a piece of creative writing.
- It is essential that pupils have access to success criteria or a mark scheme to ensure they provide feedback that is linked to the set task, and in addition to being kind, specific and helpful, the feedback should also be relevant and meaningful.
- Pupils can write their feedback on a sticky note and attach it to the classwork (again, remaining anonymous can be helpful), or they can add their comments to a feedback sheet attached to the classwork.
- Once pupils have had time to provide feedback for different pieces of work (it is unlikely that pupils will be able to comment on every piece of work within one lesson), they will then review the feedback their work has received.
- The learners should then take time to read and reflect on the feedback their peers have provided, and they should also have time to act on that feedback.

There are two key benefits of the gallery critique task. Firstly, pupils have the opportunity to view a large sample of their peers' work, in contrast to examples from just one or two individuals. They may find the variety interesting, and they may gain ideas, inspiration and a deeper understanding from doing so. Secondly, pupils can receive detailed feedback from a number of their classmates. This task can be time consuming, but if planned carefully can be very worthwhile.

SPaG watch

Spelling, punctuation and grammar (SPaG) are central to effective communication in the classroom, regardless of the subject. Metacognition is also an important feature of successful learning. By stressing the importance of certain elements of learning, such as SPaG, learners are able to ensure that they are at the front of their mind during the lesson, especially when completing a written task.

'SPaG watch' acts as a form of peer assessment or peer support. Students can volunteer for SPaG watch roles, or they can be selected by the teacher. SPaG watch involves members of the class, often one or two pupils, taking on roles to monitor the work of their peers and provide feedback with a specific focus on literacy.

Examples of this can include a 'spelling squad'. A pupil will have the designated role to check other pupils' work, but they will only focus on the spelling of key terms (they don't observe or comment on content or other aspects of literacy). This is to ensure they are only checking for spelling errors and don't get distracted by other mistakes. The pupil checking spellings can have a list of key terms to check these words are spelled correctly. They have to inform their peers if they find a spelling error when reading their work, and the spelling has to be corrected immediately.

Another key role is the 'punctuation police'; the concept is the same as for the spelling squad, but the focus is on addressing punctuation errors for their peers to rectify. This can involve punctuation in general or be more precise with a focus on the correct use of capital letters or full stops. Other areas for pupils to specialise in can include the correct use of tenses or accurate homophones.

Pupils in the SPaG watch roles don't support their peers for the duration of a lesson, as they have their own classwork to complete. There will be specific points in a lesson (which have to be after students have had sufficient time to write their responses) when the SPaG watch stand up, walk around the classroom and help their peers.

To signal the time for SPaG watch to do their job, I used to play music and the individuals would walk around the classroom scanning written responses and offering feedback as the music played. However, the music can be a distraction, so this might not be the best option; an alternative is simply for the teacher to instruct the pupils to help their classmates and advise them when to stop.

My pupils (KS3 classes) were very vocal about enjoying this activity. The pupils in the SPaG watch roles found it rewarding to be able to help their classmates, while other members of the class told me they tried harder with their written work because they knew someone would be checking it in the lesson. After sharing this idea on X, other schools adopted this for their classes and their context.

This idea has also been used in KS2, with primary teachers allowing the pupils who are on SPaG watch to wear a lanyard or sticker. History teacher Sarah Lidell at Ysgol Bryn Alyn, Wrexham, created 'grammar gangsters' and geography teacher and assistant headteacher Rhys Corcoran at Mary Immaculate High School, Cardiff, adapted this idea to use with older students, creating 'literacy leaders'. The SPaG watch activity enables pupils to support their peers and receive help from their classmates; it has a specific focus, and by pupils offering explicit feedback and instruction there can be an immediate, actionable impact.

It takes two

'It takes two' peer feedback takes paired peer assessment a step further by asking pupils to critique the work of a peer alongside their partner, so they can discuss and agree on the feedback they will provide. The following is an example of how this can work.

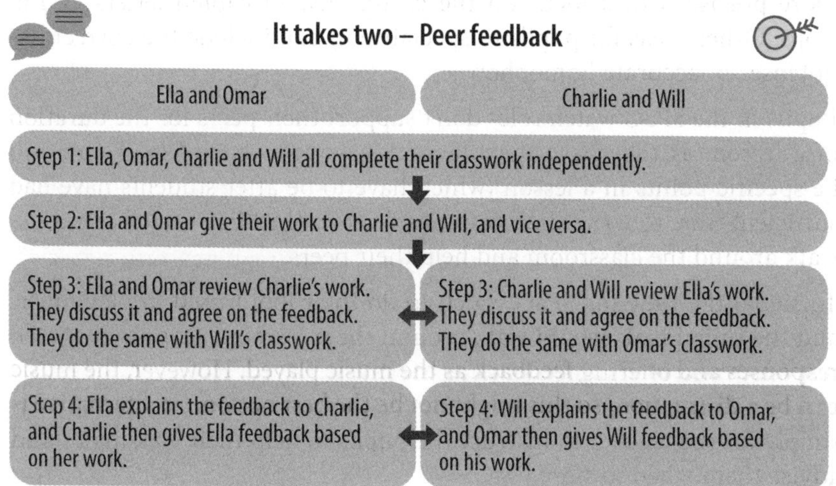

This feedback exercise can take place while a piece of work is being written or after it has been completed. Pupils are assigned to work together in pairs for this task, and each pair gives their work to another pair. The pair reads one of the pupils' pieces of work first and using the success criteria discusses what feedback they should provide.

This conversation helps the learners to reflect and verbalise their thoughts and feedback, as their partner may either agree or challenge the feedback. They both have to reach an agreement about the feedback that will be provided to the learner. Then they review the second pupil's work and do the same.

It can help if the pupils providing feedback write down their thoughts and feedback in case they forget it; this can be completed in class books or on sticky notes. The teacher sets a specific time (ensuring enough time is provided for learners to review the work and agree on the feedback), and the next step is for the feedback to be delivered. One person from each pair returns the feedback to the person in the other pair, who will then give the feedback on that person's work. The other pair will have been discussing their work, so they are providing feedback to one another.

Knowing that two individuals have agreed on the feedback provided can give the learner more trust and faith in the critique. Having the opportunity to discuss the feedback with their partner can also give the pupil more confidence about the feedback they are giving.

Chapter summary

- There are challenges involved with peer assessment, including bias, conflict, fairness and the ability to skilfully provide feedback to peers.
- The challenges can be overcome with regular training, clear instruction and guidance, in addition to monitoring and support.
- Peer assessment, as with self-assessment, should not be used for summative and high stakes assessment.
- A simple way to introduce peer assessment is through peer quizzing and scoring.
- Other methods of peer assessment include the kind, specific and helpful approach combined with feedback frames, TAG Me, gallery critique and 'it takes two'.

Final thoughts and reflections

It is clear that feedback is a crucial element of evidence-based and effective teaching and learning. It can support and enhance pupil understanding, progress and motivation. However, feedback doesn't always land the way teachers hope it will. Ensuring that feedback provided to learners is helpful and not harmful isn't always easy, but there are guiding principles all teachers can adopt and apply.

Teacher workload has been a serious and ongoing issue for years, and has not yet been resolved. Although there are various factors that contribute to workload tensions, feedback (mainly in terms of marking) is onerous, particularly in some subjects. However, feedback can be provided to learners in ways that are effective and efficient, without being a time-consuming burden.

Written feedback can be provided without lengthy and repetitive comments in individual class books. Verbal feedback can support learners of all ages and across all subjects and topics. Feedback conversations should be happening regularly at various stages of the learning process and can range from one-to-one to whole class approaches.

Peer and self-assessments are not without their challenges and limitations, but they can have many benefits such as involving pupils in the feedback process. Technology can have a negative impact on pupils' academic progress and wellbeing, so the need to monitor screen time and promote e-safety is crucial. However, as technology continues to advance, websites, apps and tools are being designed that can help to reduce teacher workload and support pupils' learning.

I hope this book has provided clarity in the complex field of feedback in education. This book provides a range of practical examples that teachers may choose to trial or implement in their classrooms. The tips and advice are offered to support teachers with existing practices, with a focus on continual development and growth. The case studies offer guidance and share reflections on practice from figures in the industry, from classroom teachers to senior leaders.

Feedback can be efficient for the teacher and effective for the pupil if the key principles and practices are followed, implemented and embedded carefully and supported by regular reflection and review.

Bibliography

Introduction

Hattie, J. and Timperley, H. (2007). 'The Power of Feedback', *Review of Educational Research* 77(1) 81–112.

Education Endowment Foundation (2021). 'Teacher Feedback to Improve Pupil Learning. Provide effective feedback to support learning'. Available at: https://educationendowmentfoundation.org.uk/education-evidence/guidance-reports/feedback

Heen, S. and Stone, D. (2015). *Thanks for the Feedback. The Science and Art of Receiving Feedback Well Even When It Is Off Base, Unfair, Poorly Delivered, and, Frankly, You're Not In The Mood.* Penguin Group USA.

Hendrick, C. and Macpherson, R. (2017). *What Does This Look Like In The Classroom? Bridging The Gap Between Research And Practice.* John Catt Publishing.

Hattie, J. (2011). From Sutton, R., Hornsey, M. J. and Douglas, K. M. (Eds., 2011). *Feedback: The communication of praise, criticism, and advice.* Peter Lang Publishing: New York.

Fawcett, D. (2019). *Relearning to Teach: Understanding the Principles of Great Teaching*, Routledge

Wiliam, D. and Leahy, S. (2015). *Embedding Formative Assessment: Practical Techniques for K-12 Classrooms.* Learning Sciences International.

Kirschner, A, P. (2018) 'No Feedback, No Learning'. Available at: https://3starlearningexperiences.wordpress.com/2018/06/05/no-feedback-no-learning/

Tharby, A. (2016). 'How to ensure that feedback leads to real learning'. Available at: https://reflectingenglish.wordpress.com/2016/01/10/how-to-ensure-that-feedback-leads-to-real-learning/

Wiggins, G. (2012). 'Seven Keys to Effective Feedback'. Available at: https://www.ascd.org/el/articles/seven-keys-to-effective-feedback

Wiliam, D. (2014). 'Is the Feedback You're Giving Students Helping or Hindering?' Available at: https://www.dylanwiliamcenter.com/2014/11/29/is-the-feedback-you-are-giving-students-helping-or-hindering/

NASUWT (n.d.). 'Tackling Excessive Teacher Workload (England and Wales). Available at: https://www.nasuwt.org.uk/advice/conditions-of-service/workload/tackling-excessive-teacher-workload-england-wales.html

DfE (2019). 'Teacher workload survey 2019. Available at: https://www.gov.uk/government/publications/teacher-workload-survey-2019

NEU (n.d.). Press releases. Available at: https://neu.org.uk/latest/press-releases

Schleicher, A. (2020). Education International, *OECD: Technology can amplify the work of great teachers, but it will not replace them*. Available at: https://www.ei-ie.org/en/item/23292:oecd-technology-can-amplify-the-work-of-great-teachers-but-it-will-not-replace-them

C, Hendrick., and Kirscher, A, P. (2024). *How Learning Happens: Seminal Works in Educational Psychology and What They Mean in Practice.* Second Edition. David Fulton.

Chapter 1 – Written feedback

Education Endowment Foundation (2021). 'Teacher Feedback to Improve Pupil Learning. Provide effective feedback to support learning'. Available at: https://educationendowmentfoundation.org.uk/education-evidence/guidance-reports/feedback

The Guardian (2013). 'The butterfly effect: Tim Brighouse on how schools could benefit from it'. Available at: https://www.theguardian.com/education/2013/sep/03/butterfly-effect-schools-nqt-teachers

Kirby, J. (2015). 'Hornets and Butterflies: How to reduce workload'. Available at: https://joe-kirby.com/2015/06/06/hornets-and-butterflies-how-to-reduce-workload/

Kirby, J. (2023). 'Hornets, Slugs, Bees and Butterflies: not-to-do lists and the workload relief revolution'. Available at: https://joe-kirby.com/2023/02/04/hornets-bees-butterflies-workload-relief-revolution/

Department for Education (2021). 'Policy paper: Early career framework'. Available at: https://assets.publishing.service.gov.uk/media/60795936d3bf7f400b462d74/Early-Career_Framework_April_2021.pdf

Hendrick, C. and Macpherson, R. (2017). *What Does This Look Like in The Classroom?: Bridging the Gap Between Research and Practice.* John Catt Publishing.

Ashman, G. (2015). 'Filling the Pail, Givers should also be receivers'. Available at: https://gregashman.wordpress.com/2015/12/07/givers-should-also-be-receivers/

Soderstrom, N. and Bjork, R. (2015). 'Learning Versus Performance: An Integrative Review'. *Perspectives on Psychological Science* 2015, Vol. 10(2) 176–199. Available at: https://bjorklab.psych.ucla.edu/wp-content/uploads/sites/13/2016/11/soderstorm_ra_learningvsperformance.pdf

McGill, R. M. (2017). *Mark. Plan. Teach. Save Time. Reduce Workload. Impact Learning.* Bloomsbury.

Durran, J. (2017). 'Marking for "literacy" – problems with "codes"'. Available at: https://jamesdurran.blog/2017/05/13/marking-for-literacy-problems-with-codes/

Fairlamb, A., innovate my school, 'Adventures in coded marking'. Available at: https://www.innovatemyschool.com/ideas/adventures-in-coded-marking

Ontario Ministry of Education (2007). 'Teacher Moderation: Collaborative Assessment of Student Work'.

TeacherToolkit (2018). 'Yellow Box Methodology'. Available at: https://www.teachertoolkit.co.uk/2018/05/19/yellow-box-methodology/

Sherrington, T. and Stafford, S., Chartered College of Teaching (2021). 'Effective feedback: Selective marking'. Available at: https://my.chartered.college/wp-content/uploads/2021/10/Selective-feedback_Sherrington.pdf

Alsop, J. (2019). 'Writus Andronicus, Quick and Effective Lesson Ideas #5 – 'The Big Yellow Box' (Or, How to make your students work harder than you!)'. Available at: https://writusandronicus.blog/2019/10/16/quick-and-effective-lesson-ideas-5-the-big-yellow-box-or-how-to-make-your-students-work-harder-than-you/

Education Scotland (2016). 'Self and peer assessment – Dylan Wiliam'. Available at: https://www.youtube.com/watch?v=YtP4X5Vls9Y

Sherrington, T., Teacherhead (2017). '#FiveWays of Giving Effective Feedback as Actions'. Available at: https://teacherhead.com/2017/12/18/fiveways-of-giving-effective-feedback-as-actions/

Christodoulou, D. (researched) (2018). 'Comparative judgement: the next big revolution in assessment?' Available at: https://researched.org.uk/2018/07/06/comparative-judgement-the-next-big-revolution-in-assessment-2/

Jones, A. C., Wardlow, L., Pan, S. C. et al. (2016). 'Beyond the Rainbow: Retrieval Practice Leads to Better Spelling than does Rainbow Writing'. *Educ Psychol Rev* 28, 385–400. Available at: https://doi.org/10.1007/s10648-015-9330-6

Puentedura, R. R. (2009). 'Learning, Technology, and the SAMR Model: Goals, Processes, and Practice'. Available at: http://www.hippasus.com/rrpweblog/archives/2014/06/29/ LearningTechnologySAMRModel.pdf

Best, J., 3P Learning (2020). 'The SAMR Model Explained (With 15 Practical Examples)'. Available at: https://www.3plearning.com/blog/connectingsamrmodel/

Kurt, S., Educational Technology (2023). *SAMR Model: Substitution, Augmentation, Modification, and Redefinition*. Available at: https://educationaltechnology.net/samr-model-substitution-augmentation-modification-and-redefinition/

Kingson, J. A., Axios (2024). 'Teachers are embracing ChatGPT-powered grading'. Available at: https://www.axios.com/2024/03/06/ai-tools-teachers-chatgpt-writable

Hamilton, A., Hattie, J. and Wiliam, D. (2023). 'The Future of AI in Education: 13 things we can do to minimize the damage'. Working paper.

Chapter 2 – Verbal feedback

Harvard Business Review, 'When to Give Verbal Feedback – and When to Do It in Writing'. Available at: https://hbr.org/2022/12/when-to-give-verbal-feedback-and-when-to-do-it-in-writing

Education Endowment Foundation (2021). 'Teacher Feedback to Improve Pupil Learning. Provide effective feedback to support learning'. Available at: https://educationendowmentfoundation.org.uk/education-evidence/guidance-reports/feedback

Van Der Kleij, F. and Adie, L. (2020). 'Towards effective feedback: an investigation of teachers' and students' perceptions of oral feedback in classroom practice'. *Assessment in Education: Principles, Policy & Practice*, 27(3), 252–270. Available at: https://doi.org/10.1080/0969594X.2020.1748871

Wiggins, G. and McTighe, J. (2005, 2nd ed.). *Understanding by Design.* Alexandria, VA: Association for Supervision and Curriculum Development ASCD.

Education Scotland, 'Dylan Wiliam: Feedback on learning'. Available at: https://www.youtube.com/watch?v=n7Ox5aoZ4ww

Jha, A. (2021). *Peak Mind: Find Your Focus, Own Your Attention, Invest 12 Minutes a Day.* Piatkus Books.

Gathercole, S. and Alloway, T. P. (2008). *Working Memory and Learning: A Practical Guide for Teachers.* SAGE Publications Ltd.

Perry, T., Lea, R., Jørgensen, C. R., Cordingley, P., Shapiro, K. and Youdell, D. (2021). *Cognitive Science in the Classroom.* London: Education Endowment Foundation.

Education Endowment Foundation. 'Early Years Toolkit'. Available at: https://educationendowmentfoundation.org.uk/education-evidence/early-years-toolkit

Department for Education, 'Early years foundation stage statutory framework'. Available at: https://assets.publishing.service.gov.uk/media/65aa5e42ed27ca001327b2c7/EYFS_statutory_framework_for_group_and_school_based_providers.pdf

McGill, R. M., TeacherToolkit (2017). 'Verbal Feedback: Research'. Available at: https://www.teachertoolkit.co.uk/2017/05/02/verbal-feedback-research/

UCL Verbal Feedback Project. Available at: https://www.ucl.ac.uk/widening-participation/teachers-and-education-professionals/teacher-research-projects/verbal-feedback-project

Flying High Partnership, 'Reducing teacher workload'. Available at: https://assets.publishing.service.gov.uk/media/5aa2a6c840f0b66b5fb4b2e1/Flying_High_-_Reducing_teacher_workload.pdf

Wiliam, D. and Leahy, S. (2015). *Embedding Formative Assessment: Practical Techniques for K-12 Classrooms.* Learning Sciences International.

Hendrick, C. and Macpherson, R. (2017). *What Does This Look Like in The Classroom?: Bridging the Gap Between Research and Practice.* John Catt Publishing.

Schoneveld, E. and Brummelman, E. (2023). '"You did incredibly well!": teachers' inflated praise can make children from low-SES backgrounds seem less smart (but more hardworking)'. *npj Sci. Learn.* 8, 31. Available at: https://doi.org/10.1038/s41539-023-00183-w

Burnett, P. C. (2010). 'Praise and Feedback in the Primary Classroom: Teachers' and Students' Perspectives'. Available at: https://www.researchgate.net/publication/228359095_Praise_and_Feedback_in_the_Primary_Classroom_Teachers'_and_Students'_Perspectives

Lemov, D. (2021). *Teach Like a Champion 3.0: 63 Techniques that Put Students on the Path to College.* Jossey-Bass.

Teacher Tapp (n.d.). Available at: https://teachertapp.co.uk/

McGee, N. (2021). Available at: https://x.com/RE_McGEE/status/1459972476277080064

TeacherToolkit (2018). 'Educational Fad: Verbal Feedback Stamps'. Available at: https://www.teachertoolkit.co.uk/2018/07/15/educational-fad-14/

TeacherToolkit (2015). 'Verbal Feedback Stamp Madness!' Available at: https://www.teachertoolkit.co.uk/2015/09/27/verbal-feedback-stamp-madness/

Education Endowment Foundation (2020). 'Special Educational Needs in Mainstream Schools'. Available at: https://educationendowmentfoundation.org.uk/education-evidence/guidance-reports/send

Wespieser, K. (ed.), researchED series (2021). *The researchED Guide to Special Educational Needs: An evidence-informed guide for teachers.* John Catt Publishing.

REAL Learners. 'Written feedback to support EAL learners: does it help when you don't know what you don't know?' Available at: https://www.reallearners.co.uk/written-feedback-to-support-eal-learners-does-it-help-when-you-dont-know-what-you-dont-know/

Hartshorn, K. James and Evans, N. W. (2015). 'The Effects of Dynamic Written Corrective Feedback: A 30-Week Study', *Journal of Response to Writing*: Vol. 1: Iss. 2, Article 2. Available at: https://scholarsarchive.byu.edu/journalrw/vol1/iss2/2

Truscott, J. (2020). 'The efficacy of written corrective feedback: A critique of a meta-analysis.' Unpublished manuscript. National Tsing Hua University.

Camerer, C., Loewenstein, G. and Weber, M. (1989). 'The curse of knowledge in economic settings: An experimental analysis'. *Journal of Political Economy*, 97(5), 1232–1254. Available at: https://doi.org/10.1086/261651

Heath C. and Heath D. (2007, 1st ed.). *Made to stick: Why some ideas survive and others die.* Random House.

Chapter 3 – Whole class feedback

Hattie, J. (2011). From Sutton, R., Hornsey, M. J. and Douglas, K. M. (Eds, 2011). *Feedback: The communication of praise, criticism, and advice.* Peter Lang Publishing, New York. Available at: https://www.visiblelearning.com/sites/default/files/Feedback%20article.pdf

Christodoulou, D. (2018). 'Comparative judgement: the next big revolution in assessment?'. Available at: https://researched.org.uk/2018/07/06/comparative-judgement-the-next-big-revolution-in-assessment-2/

Mccrea, P. 'Flipping failure: Building scholarly identity'. Available at: https://snacks.pepsmccrea.com/p/flipping-failure

Hendrick, C. and Macpherson, R. (2017). *What Does This Look Like in The Classroom?: Bridging the Gap Between Research and Practice.* John Catt Publishing.

mrthorntonteach. 'Marking Crib Sheet & Whole Class Feedback'. Available at: https://mrthorntonteach.com/2016/04/08/marking-crib-sheet/

Kirby, J. (2017). 'Three Assessment Butterflies'. Available at: https://joe-kirby.com/2017/07/01/three-assessment-butterflies/

Harford, S. (2016). 'Marking and other myths'. Available at: https://educationinspection.blog.gov.uk/2016/11/28/marking-and-other-myths/

Hill, C. (2017). 'Research: the gift of time'. Available at: https://aclassroomofonesownsite.wordpress.com/2017/09/16/research-the-gift-of-time/

Law, S., Huntington Research School (2021). 'Whole Class Feedback: a primary case study'. Available at: https://researchschool.org.uk/huntington/news/whole-class-feedback-a-primary-case-study

MACS Teaching & Learning. 'Whole Class Feedback'. Available at: https://macstandl.com/whole-class-feedback/

Riches, A., TES Magazine (2019). 'Pedagogy Focus: Peer assessment'. Available at: https://www.tes.com/magazine/archive/whole-class-feedback-fad-or-workload-saviour

Brown, A. L. and Campione, J. C. (1996). 'Psychological theory and the design of innovative learning environments: On procedures, principles, and systems' in Schauble, L. and Glaser, R. (Eds). *Innovations in learning: New environments for education* (pp. 289–325). Hillsdale, NJ: Lawrence Erlbaum Associates.

Boxer, A. (2018). 'A Chemical Orthodoxy, 7 simple ways to encourage metacognition in the science classroom'. Available at: https://achemicalorthodoxy.co.uk/2018/06/18/7-simple-ways-to-encourage-metacognition-in-the-science-classroom/

Wiliam, D. and Leahy, S. (2015). *Embedding Formative Assessment: Practical Techniques for K-12 Classrooms.* Learning Sciences International.

Chapter 4 – Self-assessment

Jones, K. (2021). *Wiliam & Leahy's Five Formative Assessment Strategies in Action.* John Catt Publishing.

Sadler, D. Royce (1989). 'Formative assessment and the design of instructional systems'. *Instructional Science*, 18, 119–144.

Chin, P. (2016). 'Peer assessment'. *New Directions in the Teaching of Natural Sciences*, (3), 13–18. Available at: https://doi.org/10.29311/ndtps.v0i3.410

Education Endowment Foundation (2018). 'Metacognition and Self-regulated Learning: Guidance Report'. Available at: https://educationendowmentfoundation.org.uk/education-evidence/guidance-reports/metacognition

Hattie, J. and Timperley, H. (2007). 'The Power of Feedback'. *Review of Educational Research*, 77(1) 81–112.

Hattie, J. (2011). From Sutton, R., Hornsey, M. J. and Douglas, K. M. (Eds) (2011). *Feedback: The communication of praise, criticism, and advice.* Peter Lang Publishing, New York. Available at: https://www.visiblelearning.com/sites/default/files/Feedback%20article.pdf

De Bruyckere, P. (2018). *The Ingredients for Great Teaching.* Sage Publications.

Hendrick, C. (2017). Interview with Dylan Wiliam. Available at: https://carlhendrick.com/2017/09/02/four-quarters-marking-a-workload-solution/

Chiles, M. (2020). *The Feedback Pendulum: A Manifesto for Enhancing Feedback in Education.* John Catt Publishing.

Hendrick, C. and Macpherson, R. (2017). *What Does This Look Like in The Classroom?: Bridging the Gap Between Research and Practice.* John Catt Publishing.

Fawcett, D. (2019). *Relearning to Teach: Understanding the Principles of Great Teaching.* Routledge.

Ali, A., Try This Teaching (2014). 'Dot Marking'. Available at: https://www.trythisteaching.com/2014/06/dot-marking/

Bjork, R. A. and Bjork, E. L. (1992). 'A new theory of disuse and an old theory of stimulus fluctuation'. In Healy, A., Kosslyn, S. and Shiffrin, R. (Eds). *From learning processes to cognitive processes: Essays in honor of William K. Estes* (Vol. 2, pp. 35–67). Hillsdale, NJ: Erlbaum.

Bjork, E. L. and Bjork, R. A. (2011). 'Making things hard on yourself, but in a good way: Creating desirable difficulties to enhance learning'. In Gernsbacher, M. A., Pew, R. W., Hough, L. M. and Pomerantz, J. R, (Eds)

and FABBS Foundation. *Psychology and the real world: Essays illustrating fundamental contributions to society* (pp. 56–64). Worth Publishers.

Kirschner, P. A., Sweller, J. and Clark, R. E. (2006). 'Why Minimal Guidance During Instruction Does Not Work: An Analysis of the Failure of Constructivist, Discovery, Problem-Based, Experiential, and Inquiry-Based Teaching'. *Educational Psychologist*, 41(2), 75–86. Available at: https://doi.org/10.1207/s15326985ep4102_1

'C-Scores: Using Responsive Quizzing'. Available at: https://carousel-learning.zendesk.com/hc/en-gb/articles/12209854647442-C-Scores-Using-Responsive-Quizzing

Teach Like a Champion, Doug Lemov's Field Notes. (2014). 'The Do Now: A Primer'. Available at: https://teachlikeachampion.org/blog/now-primer/

Allan, C., Castelino, J., Millichamp, T., Robbins, A. and Wilkinson, B, Series Editor: Boxer, A. (2024). *Springboard KS3 Science Knowledge Book* (2024). Hodder Education.

Kirby, J. (2015). 'Knowledge Organisers'. Avaible at: https://joe-kirby.com/2015/03/28/knowledge-organisers/

Kaplan, M., Silver, N., LaVaque-Manty, D. and Meizlish, D. (2013). *Using Reflection and Metacognition to Improve Student Learning: Across the Disciplines, Across the Academy.* Stylus.

Quigley, A. 'Top 10 Revision Strategies'. Available at: https://www.theconfidentteacher.com/2018/01/top-10-revision-strategies/

Education Endowment Foundation (2018). 'Metacognition and Self-regulated Learning. Apply metacognitive strategies in the classroom'. Available at: https://educationendowmentfoundation.org.uk/education-evidence/guidance-reports/metacognition

Coe, R., Rauch, C. J., Kime, S. and Singleton, D., Evidence Based Education (2020). 'Great teaching toolkit: Evidence Review'.

Sebesta, A. J. and Speth, E. B. (2017). 'How should I study for the exam? Self-regulated learning strategies and achievement in introductory biology'. *CBE Life Sciences Education*, 16(2). Available at: https://doi.org/10.1187/cbe.16-09-0269

Chapter 5 – Peer assessment

Chin, P. (2016). 'Peer assessment'. *New Directions in the Teaching of Natural Sciences*, (3), 13–18. Available at: https://doi.org/10.29311/ndtps.v0i3.410

TES Magazine, 'Pedagogy Focus: Peer assessment'. Available at: https://www.tes.com/magazine/archive/pedagogy-focus-peer-assessment

Chan C. (2010). 'Assessment: Self and Peer Assessment'. Assessment Resources@HKU, University of Hong Kong. Available at: https://ar.talic.hku.hk/self_peer.htm

Falchikov, N. and Goldfinch, J. (2000). 'Student peer assessment in higher education: A meta-analysis comparing peer and teacher marks'. *Review of Educational Research*, 70(3) 287–322.

Carvalho, A. (2023). *Students' perceptions of fairness in peer assessment: Evidence from a problem-based learning course.* Teaching in Higher Education.

Wiliam, D. and Leahy, S. (2015). *Embedding Formative Assessment: Practical Techniques for K-12 Classrooms.* Learning Sciences International.

Stonewall, J. H., Dorneich, M. C. and Rongerude, J. (2024). 'Training to increase student perceptions of fairness in peer assessment'. *Assessment & Evaluation in Higher Education*, 1–17. Available at: https://doi.org/10.1080/02602938.2024.2327858

Quigley, A., TES Magazine (2024). 'How to get peer assessment right'. Available at: https://www.tes.com/magazine/teaching-learning/general/how-teachers-can-use-peer-feedback-and-assessment

Berger, R. (2003). *An Ethic of Excellence. Building a Culture of Craftsmanship with Students.* Heinemann Educational Books, US.

Hendrick, C. and Macpherson, R. (2017). *What Does This Look Like in The Classroom?: Bridging the Gap Between Research and Practice.* John Catt Publishing.

Chiles, M. (2020). *The Feedback Pendulum: A Manifesto for Enhancing Feedback in Education.* John Catt Publishing.

Education Scotland. 'Dylan Wiliam – Self and peer assessment'. (2017) Available at: https://education.gov.scot/resources/dylan-wiliam-self-and-peer-assessment/

Ferguson, M. (2023). *See One, Do One, Teach One: 12 lessons to support GCSE English*, John Catt Publishing.

Class Teaching (2015). 'Gallery Critique'. Available at: https://classteaching.wordpress.com/2015/06/04/gallery-critique/

Hare, T., The Art of Education University (2015). 'An Engaging Critique That Taps into Your Students' Love of Quick Communication'. Available at: https://theartofeducation.edu/2015/10/an-engaging-critique-that-taps-into-your-students-love-of-quick-communication/

Jones, K. and Wiliam, D., ASCD (2021). 'Getting the "Think-Pair-Share" Technique Right'. Available at: https://www.ascd.org/blogs/getting-the-think-pair-share-technique-right